$(1+x)^{3}$.

$a = 1$
$b = x$
$n = 3$

$(a+b)^{n} = a^{n} + \binom{n}{1} a^{n-1} b + \binom{n}{2} a^{n-1} b^{2} + \frac{n}{3} a^{n-1/3} b +$

$= 1 + \binom{3}{1} a^{3-1}(x) + \binom{3}{2} 1^{2} x^{2} + \binom{3}{3} 1^{3} x^{3}$

AS Maths

AQA Core 2

AS level maths is seriously tricky — no question about that.

We've done everything we can to make things easier for you.
We've scrutinised past paper questions and we've gone through the syllabuses with a
fine-toothed comb. So we've found out exactly what you need to know, then
explained it simply and clearly.

We've stuck in as many helpful hints as you could possibly want
— then we even tried to put some funny bits in to keep you awake.

We've done our bit — the rest is up to you.

What CGP is all about

Our sole aim here at CGP is to produce the highest quality
books — carefully written, immaculately presented and
dangerously close to being funny.

Then we work our socks off to get them out to you
— at the cheapest possible prices.

Contents

SECTION 6 — INTEGRATION

P1 — PRACTICE EXAM 1

P1 — PRACTICE EXAM 2

This book covers the Core 2 module of the AQA specification.

Published by Coordination Group Publications Ltd.

Contributors:
Charley Darbishire
Simon Little
Andy Park
Glenn Rogers
Claire Thompson

And:
Bill Dolling
Dave Harding
Mark Moody
Iain Nash
Mike Smith
Caroline Starkey
Kieran Wardell

Updated by:
Alison Chisolm
Tim Major
Sam Norman
Andy Park
Alan Rix
Claire Thompson
Mark Turner
Julie Wakeling

ISBN: 978 1 84146 767 2

Groovy website: www.cgpbooks.co.uk

Jolly bits of clipart from CorelDRAW®
With thanks to Colin Wells and Christine Nicholson for the proofreading.

Printed by Elanders Hindson Ltd, Newcastle upon Tyne.

Laws of Indices

You use the laws of indices a helluva lot in maths — when you're integrating, differentiating and ...er... well loads of other places. So take the time to get them sorted now.

Three mega-important Laws of Indices

You must know these three rules. I can't make it any clearer than that.

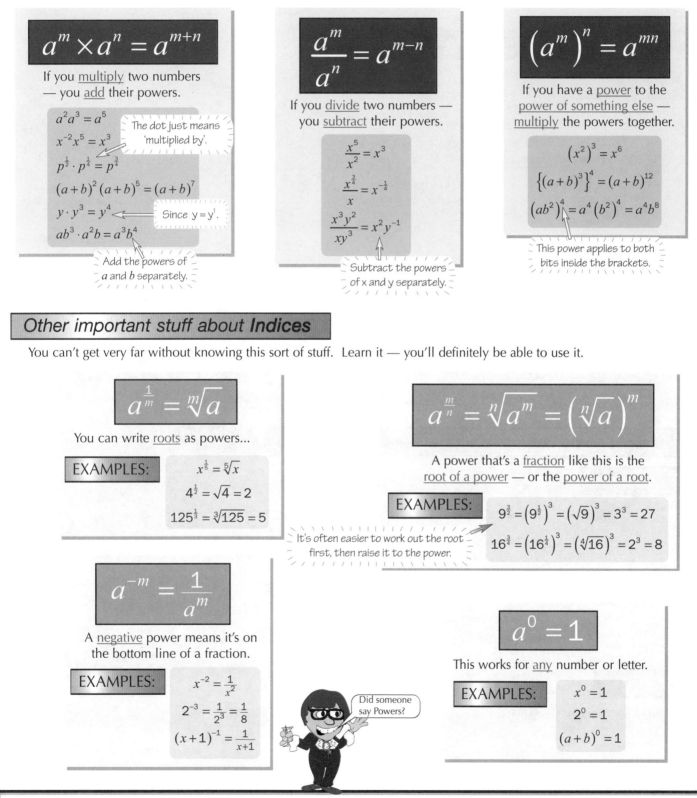

$$a^m \times a^n = a^{m+n}$$

If you multiply two numbers — you add their powers.

$a^2 a^3 = a^5$

$x^{-2} x^5 = x^3$ ← The dot just means 'multiplied by'.

$p^{\frac{1}{2}} \cdot p^{\frac{1}{4}} = p^{\frac{3}{4}}$

$(a+b)^2 (a+b)^5 = (a+b)^7$

$y \cdot y^3 = y^4$ ← Since $y = y^1$.

$ab^3 \cdot a^2 b = a^3 b^4$

Add the powers of a and b separately.

$$\frac{a^m}{a^n} = a^{m-n}$$

If you divide two numbers — you subtract their powers.

$\dfrac{x^5}{x^2} = x^3$

$\dfrac{x^{\frac{3}{4}}}{x} = x^{-\frac{1}{4}}$

$\dfrac{x^3 y^2}{xy^3} = x^2 y^{-1}$

Subtract the powers of x and y separately.

$$\left(a^m\right)^n = a^{mn}$$

If you have a power to the power of something else — multiply the powers together.

$\left(x^2\right)^3 = x^6$

$\left\{(a+b)^3\right\}^4 = (a+b)^{12}$

$\left(ab^2\right)^4 = a^4 \left(b^2\right)^4 = a^4 b^8$

This power applies to both bits inside the brackets.

Other important stuff about Indices

You can't get very far without knowing this sort of stuff. Learn it — you'll definitely be able to use it.

$$a^{\frac{1}{m}} = \sqrt[m]{a}$$

You can write roots as powers...

EXAMPLES:

$x^{\frac{1}{5}} = \sqrt[5]{x}$

$4^{\frac{1}{2}} = \sqrt{4} = 2$

$125^{\frac{1}{3}} = \sqrt[3]{125} = 5$

It's often easier to work out the root first, then raise it to the power.

$$a^{\frac{m}{n}} = \sqrt[n]{a^m} = \left(\sqrt[n]{a}\right)^m$$

A power that's a fraction like this is the root of a power — or the power of a root.

EXAMPLES:

$9^{\frac{3}{2}} = \left(9^{\frac{1}{2}}\right)^3 = \left(\sqrt{9}\right)^3 = 3^3 = 27$

$16^{\frac{3}{4}} = \left(16^{\frac{1}{4}}\right)^3 = \left(\sqrt[4]{16}\right)^3 = 2^3 = 8$

$$a^{-m} = \frac{1}{a^m}$$

A negative power means it's on the bottom line of a fraction.

EXAMPLES:

$x^{-2} = \dfrac{1}{x^2}$

$2^{-3} = \dfrac{1}{2^3} = \dfrac{1}{8}$

$(x+1)^{-1} = \dfrac{1}{x+1}$

Did someone say Powers?

$$a^0 = 1$$

This works for any number or letter.

EXAMPLES:

$x^0 = 1$

$2^0 = 1$

$(a+b)^0 = 1$

Indices, indices — de fish all live indices...

What can I say that I haven't said already? Blah, blah, important. Blah, blah, learn these. Blah, blah, use them all the time. Mmm, that's about all that needs to be said really. So I'll be quiet and let you get on with what you need to do.

Graph Transformations

Suppose you start with any old function f(x). Then you can <u>transform</u> (change) it in three ways — by <u>translating</u> it, <u>stretching</u> or <u>reflecting</u> it.

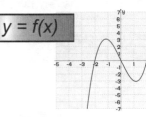

I'll use this graph of y = f(x) as an example, where
f(x) = x(x + 2)(x − 2),
i.e. f(x) = x³ − 4x.

Translations are caused by Adding things

y = f(x) + a

<u>Adding</u> a number to the <u>whole function</u> shifts the graph <u>up or down</u>.

1) If a > 0, the graph goes <u>upwards</u>.

2) If a < 0, the graph goes <u>downwards</u>.

The green graph is y = x(x + 2)(x − 2) + 2,
i.e. y = x³ − 4x + 2.

The blue graph is y = x(x + 2)(x − 2) − 4,
i.e. y = x³ − 4x − 4.

y = f(x + a)

Writing 'x + a' instead of 'x' means the graph moves <u>sideways</u>.

1) If a > 0, the graph goes to the <u>left</u>.

2) If a < 0, the graph goes to the <u>right</u>.

The green graph is y = (x − 1)³ − 4(x − 1),
i.e. y = x³ − 3x² − x + 3.

The blue graph is y = (x + 2)³ − 4(x + 2),
i.e. y = x³ + 6x² + 8x.

Stretches and Reflections are caused by Multiplying things

y = af(x)

<u>Multiplying</u> the <u>whole function</u> <u>stretches</u>, <u>squeezes</u> or <u>reflects</u> the graph <u>vertically</u>.

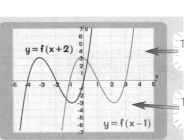

1) <u>Negative</u> values of 'a' <u>reflect</u> the basic shape in the <u>x-axis</u>.

|a| means the <u>size</u> of a, ignoring + or − signs. E.g. |4| = |−4| = 4

2) If a > 1 or a < −1 (i.e. |a| > 1) the graph is <u>stretched vertically</u>.

3) If −1 < a < 1 (i.e. |a| < 1) the graph is <u>squashed vertically</u>.

The green graph is y = −2x(x + 2)(x − 2),
i.e. y = −2x³ + 8x.

The blue graph is y = $\frac{1}{3}$x(x + 2)(x − 2),
i.e. y = $\frac{1}{3}$x³ − $\frac{4}{3}$x.

y = f(ax)

Writing 'ax' instead of 'x' <u>stretches</u>, <u>squeezes</u> or <u>reflects</u> the graph <u>horizontally</u>.

1) <u>Negative</u> values of 'a' <u>reflect</u> the basic shape in the <u>y-axis</u>.

2) If a > 1 or a < −1 (i.e. if |a| > 1) the graph is <u>squashed horizontally</u>.

3) If −1 < a < 1 (i.e. if |a| < 1) the graph is <u>stretched horizontally</u>.

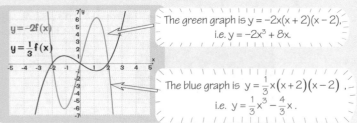

The green graph is y = $\frac{x}{2}$$\left(\frac{x}{2} + 2\right)\left(\frac{x}{2} − 2\right)$,
i.e. y = $\frac{x^3}{8}$ − 2x.

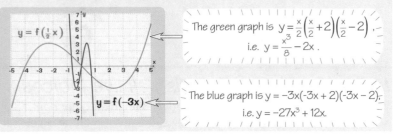

The blue graph is y = −3x(−3x + 2)(−3x − 2),
i.e. y = −27x³ + 12x.

Section One Revision Questions

And that was Section One ladies and gentlemen — short and sweet. (Well... I say sweet...)

Make sure you can answer all these questions before you move on to Section Two, though. If you can't do the basic stuff you'll be up s... ahem... you'll struggle come exam time.

1) Simplify these:

   a) $x^3.x^5$ b) $a^7.a^8$ c) $\dfrac{x^8}{x^2}$ d) $\left(a^2\right)^4$ e) $\left(xy^2\right).\left(x^3yz\right)$ f) $\dfrac{a^2b^4c^6}{a^3b^2c}$

2) Work out the following:

   a) $16^{\frac{1}{2}}$ b) $8^{\frac{1}{3}}$ c) $16^{\frac{3}{4}}$ d) x^0 e) $49^{-\frac{1}{2}}$

3) Right — now it's time to get serious. Put your thinking head on, and use the graph of f(x) to sketch what these graphs would look like after they've been 'transformed'.

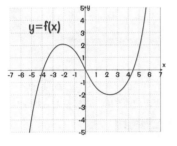

   a) $y = f(ax)$,   where (i) $a > 1$,
                                      (ii) $0 < a < 1$,
   b) $y = af(x)$,   where (i) $a > 1$,
                                      (ii) $0 < a < 1$,
   c) (i) $y = f(x + a)$,   (ii) $y = f(x - a)$,   where $a > 0$,
   d) (i) $y = f(x) + a$,   (ii) $y = f(x) - a$,   where $a > 0$.

Arc Length and Sector Area

Arc lengths and sector areas are easier than you'd think — once you've learnt two simple(ish) formulas.

Always work in **Radians** for **Arc Length** and **Sector Area** Questions

Remember — for arc length and sector area questions you've got to measure all the angles in radians.

The main thing is that you know how radians relate to degrees.

In short, 180 degrees = π radians. The table below shows you how to convert between the two units:

Converting angles	
Radians to degrees:	Degrees to radians:
Divide by π, multiply by 180.	Divide by 180, multiply by π.

Here's a table of some of the common angles you're going to need — in degrees and radians:

Degrees	0	30	45	60	90	120	180	270	360
Radians	0	$\dfrac{\pi}{6}$	$\dfrac{\pi}{4}$	$\dfrac{\pi}{3}$	$\dfrac{\pi}{2}$	$\dfrac{2\pi}{3}$	π	$\dfrac{3\pi}{2}$	2π

If you have part of a circle (like a section of pie chart), you can work out the length of the curved side, or the area of the 'slice of pie' — as long as you know the angle at the centre (θ) and the length of the radius (r). Read on...

You can find the **Length** of an **Arc** using a nice easy formula...

For a circle with a radius of r, where the angle θ is measured in radians, the arc length of the sector L is given by:

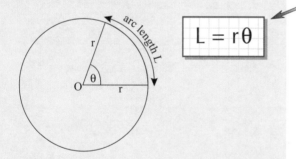

$$L = r\theta$$

If you put $\theta = 2\pi$ in this formula (and so make the sector equal to the whole circle), you get that the distance all the way round the outside of the circle is L = $2\pi r$.

This is just the normal circumference formula.

...and the area of a **Sector** using a similar formula

For a circle with a radius of r, where the angle θ is measured in radians, you can work out A, the area of the sector, using:

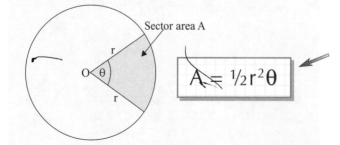

Sector area A

$$A = \tfrac{1}{2}r^2\theta$$

Again, if you put $\theta = 2\pi$ in the formula, you find that the area of the whole circle is A = $\tfrac{1}{2}r^2 \times 2\pi = \pi r^2$.

This is just the normal 'area of a circle' formula.

Arc Length and Sector Area

Questions on trigonometry quite often use the same angles — so it makes life easier if you know the sin, cos and tan of these commonly used angles. Or to put it another way, examiners expect you to know them — so learn them.

Draw Triangles to remember sin, cos and tan of the Important Angles

You should know the values of sin, cos and tan at 30°, 60° and 45°. But to help you remember, you can draw these two groovy triangles. It may seem a complicated way to learn a few numbers, but it does make it easier. Honest.

The idea is you draw the triangles below, putting in their angles and side lengths. Then you can use them to work out special trig values like sin 45° or cos 60° more accurately than any calculator (which only gives a few decimal places).

Half an equilateral triangle with sides of length 2.

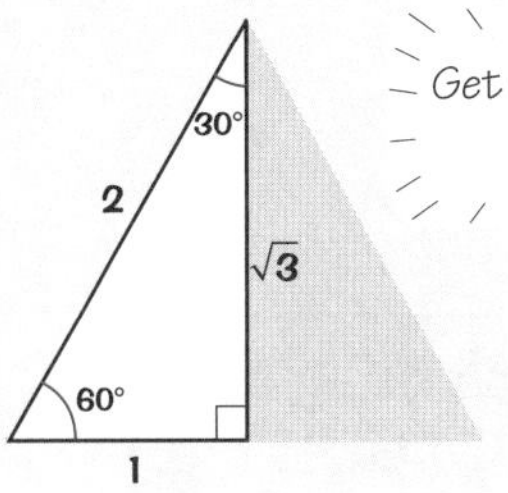

Get the height $\sqrt{3}$ by Pythagoras' Theorem: $1^2 + (\sqrt{3})^2 = 2^2$.

Then you can use the triangle to work out sin, cos and tan of 30° and 60°.

Right-angled triangle with two sides of length 1.

The $\sqrt{2}$ just comes from Pythagoras.

This triangle gives you sin, cos and tan of 45°.

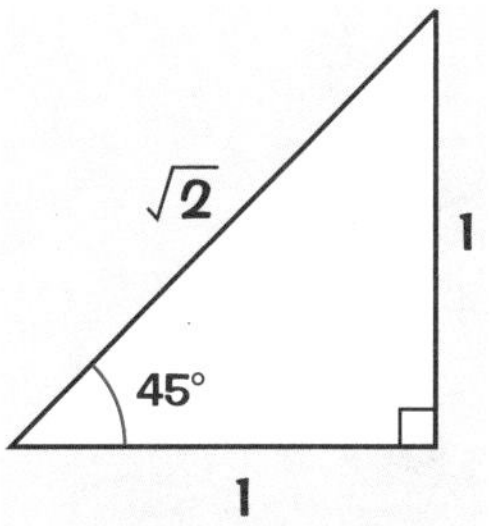

Remember: SOH CAH TOA...

$$\sin = \frac{\text{opp}}{\text{hyp}} \qquad \cos = \frac{\text{adj}}{\text{hyp}} \qquad \tan = \frac{\text{opp}}{\text{adj}}$$

Trig Values from Triangles

$\sin 30° = \frac{1}{2}$	$\sin 60° = \frac{\sqrt{3}}{2}$	$\sin 45° = \frac{1}{\sqrt{2}}$
$\cos 30° = \frac{\sqrt{3}}{2}$	$\cos 60° = \frac{1}{2}$	$\cos 45° = \frac{1}{\sqrt{2}}$
$\tan 30° = \frac{1}{\sqrt{3}}$	$\tan 60° = \sqrt{3}$	$\tan 45° = 1$

Example: Find the exact length L and area A in the diagram.

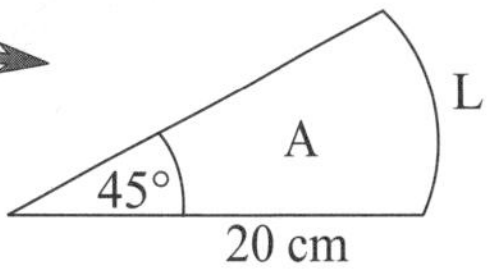

Right, first things first... it's an arc length and sector area, so you need the angle in radians.

$$45° = \frac{45 \times \pi}{180} = \frac{\pi}{4} \text{ radians}$$

Or you could just quote this if you've learnt the stuff above.

Now bung everything in your formulas:

$$L = r\theta = 20 \times \frac{\pi}{4} = 5\pi \text{ cm}$$

$$A = \frac{1}{2}r^2\theta = \frac{1}{2} \times 20^2 \times \frac{\pi}{4} = 50\pi \text{ cm}^2$$

Example: Find the area of the shaded part of the symbol.

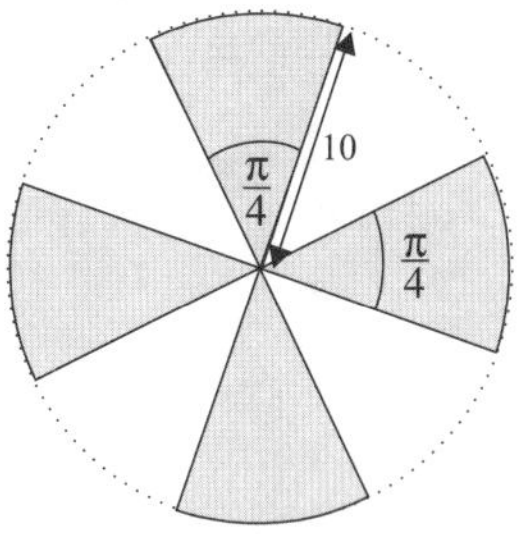

You need the area of the 'leaves' and so use the formula $\frac{1}{2}r^2\theta$.

Each leaf has area $\frac{1}{2} \times 10^2 \times \frac{\pi}{4} = 25\frac{\pi}{2} \text{ cm}^2$

So the area of the whole symbol $= 4 \times 25\frac{\pi}{2} = 50\pi \text{ cm}^2$

$\boldsymbol{\pi} = 3.14159265358979323846264338327950288419716939...$ *(Make sure you know it)*
It's worth repeating, just to make sure — those formulas for arc length and sector area only work if the angle is in radians.

The Trig Formulas You Need to Know

There are some more trig formulas you need to know for the exam.
So here they are — learn them or you're seriously stuffed. Worse than an aubergine.

The **Sine Rule** and **Cosine Rule** work for **Any** triangle

Remember these three formulas work for <u>ANY</u> triangle, not just right-angled ones.

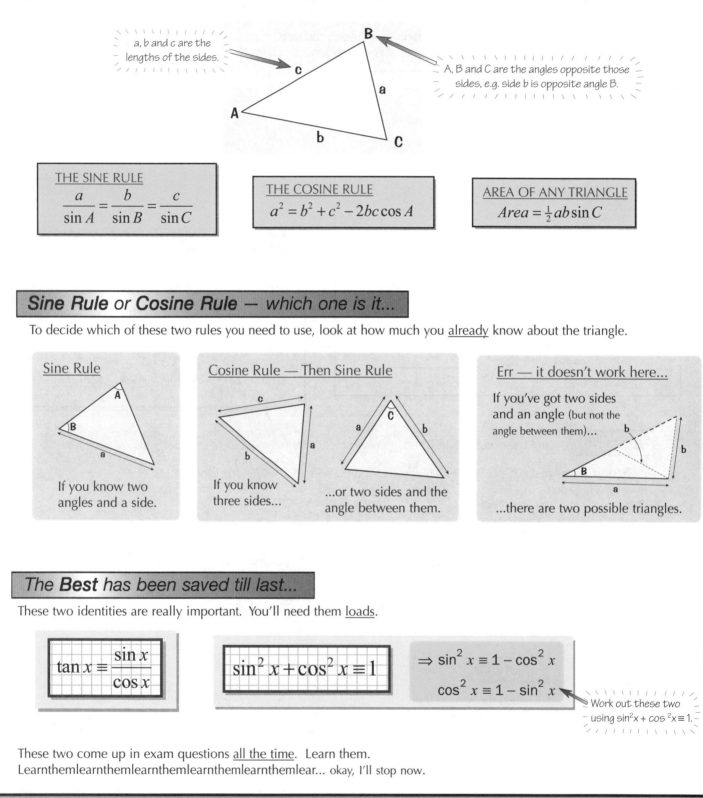

a, b and c are the lengths of the sides.

A, B and C are the angles opposite those sides, e.g. side b is opposite angle B.

THE SINE RULE
$$\frac{a}{\sin A} = \frac{b}{\sin B} = \frac{c}{\sin C}$$

THE COSINE RULE
$$a^2 = b^2 + c^2 - 2bc \cos A$$

AREA OF ANY TRIANGLE
$$Area = \tfrac{1}{2} ab \sin C$$

Sine Rule or Cosine Rule — which one is it...

To decide which of these two rules you need to use, look at how much you <u>already</u> know about the triangle.

<u>Sine Rule</u>

If you know two angles and a side.

<u>Cosine Rule — Then Sine Rule</u>

If you know three sides...

...or two sides and the angle between them.

<u>Err — it doesn't work here...</u>

If you've got two sides and an angle (but not the angle between them)...

...there are two possible triangles.

The **Best** has been saved till last...

These two identities are really important. You'll need them <u>loads</u>.

$$\tan x \equiv \frac{\sin x}{\cos x}$$

$$\sin^2 x + \cos^2 x \equiv 1$$

$$\Rightarrow \sin^2 x \equiv 1 - \cos^2 x$$
$$\cos^2 x \equiv 1 - \sin^2 x$$

Work out these two using $\sin^2 x + \cos^2 x \equiv 1$.

These two come up in exam questions <u>all the time</u>. Learn them.
Learnthemlearnthemlearnthemlearnthemlearnthemlear... okay, I'll stop now.

Tri angles — go on... you might like them.

Formulas and trigonometry go together even better than Richard and Judy. I can count 7 on this page. That's not many, so please, just make sure you know them! If you haven't learned them I will cry for you. I will sob.

Using the Sine and Cosine Rules

This page is about "solving" triangles, which just means finding all their sides and angles when you already know a few.

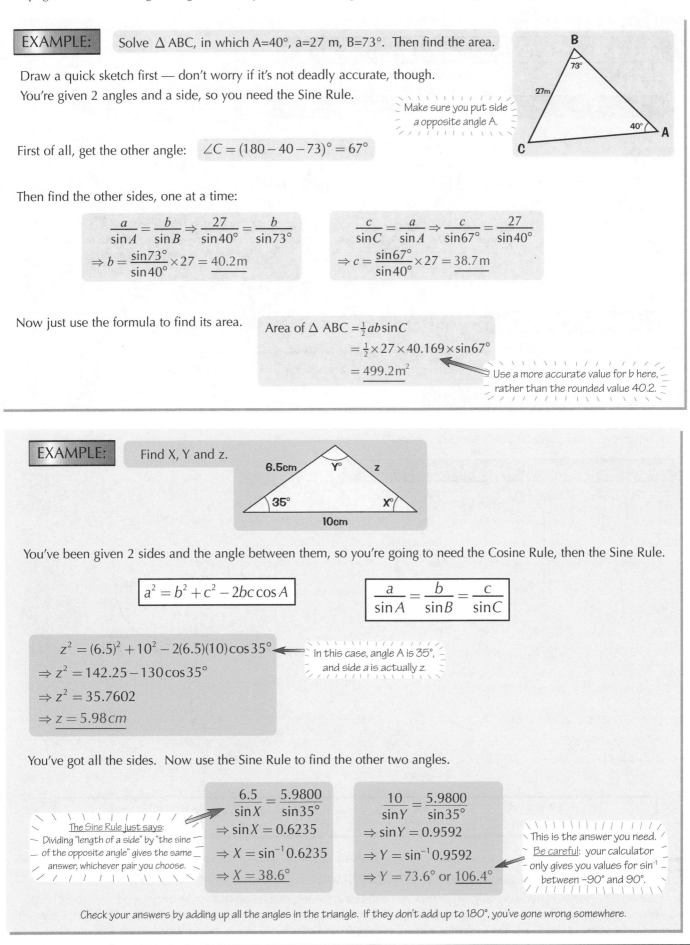

EXAMPLE: Solve △ABC, in which A=40°, a=27 m, B=73°. Then find the area.

Draw a quick sketch first — don't worry if it's not deadly accurate, though.
You're given 2 angles and a side, so you need the Sine Rule.

Make sure you put side a opposite angle A.

First of all, get the other angle: $\angle C = (180 - 40 - 73)° = 67°$

Then find the other sides, one at a time:

$$\frac{a}{\sin A} = \frac{b}{\sin B} \Rightarrow \frac{27}{\sin 40°} = \frac{b}{\sin 73°}$$
$$\Rightarrow b = \frac{\sin 73°}{\sin 40°} \times 27 = \underline{40.2\,m}$$

$$\frac{c}{\sin C} = \frac{a}{\sin A} \Rightarrow \frac{c}{\sin 67°} = \frac{27}{\sin 40°}$$
$$\Rightarrow c = \frac{\sin 67°}{\sin 40°} \times 27 = \underline{38.7\,m}$$

Now just use the formula to find its area.

$$\text{Area of } \triangle ABC = \tfrac{1}{2}ab\sin C$$
$$= \tfrac{1}{2} \times 27 \times 40.169 \times \sin 67°$$
$$= \underline{499.2\,m^2}$$

Use a more accurate value for b here, rather than the rounded value 40.2.

EXAMPLE: Find X, Y and z.

You've been given 2 sides and the angle between them, so you're going to need the Cosine Rule, then the Sine Rule.

$$a^2 = b^2 + c^2 - 2bc\cos A \qquad \frac{a}{\sin A} = \frac{b}{\sin B} = \frac{c}{\sin C}$$

$$z^2 = (6.5)^2 + 10^2 - 2(6.5)(10)\cos 35°$$
$$\Rightarrow z^2 = 142.25 - 130\cos 35°$$
$$\Rightarrow z^2 = 35.7602$$
$$\Rightarrow z = \underline{5.98\,cm}$$

In this case, angle A is 35°, and side a is actually z.

You've got all the sides. Now use the Sine Rule to find the other two angles.

The Sine Rule just says: Dividing "length of a side" by "the sine of the opposite angle" gives the same answer, whichever pair you choose.

$$\frac{6.5}{\sin X} = \frac{5.9800}{\sin 35°}$$
$$\Rightarrow \sin X = 0.6235$$
$$\Rightarrow X = \sin^{-1} 0.6235$$
$$\Rightarrow \underline{X = 38.6°}$$

$$\frac{10}{\sin Y} = \frac{5.9800}{\sin 35°}$$
$$\Rightarrow \sin Y = 0.9592$$
$$\Rightarrow Y = \sin^{-1} 0.9592$$
$$\Rightarrow Y = 73.6° \text{ or } \underline{106.4°}$$

This is the answer you need. Be careful: your calculator only gives you values for $\sin^{-1}$ between −90° and 90°.

Check your answers by adding up all the angles in the triangle. If they don't add up to 180°, you've gone wrong somewhere.

Graphs of Trig Functions

Before you leave this page, you should be able to close your eyes and picture these three graphs in your head, properly labelled and everything. If you can't, you need to learn them more. I'm not kidding.

sin x and *cos x* are always in the range *–1 to 1*

sin x and cos x are similar — they just bob up and down between –1 and 1.

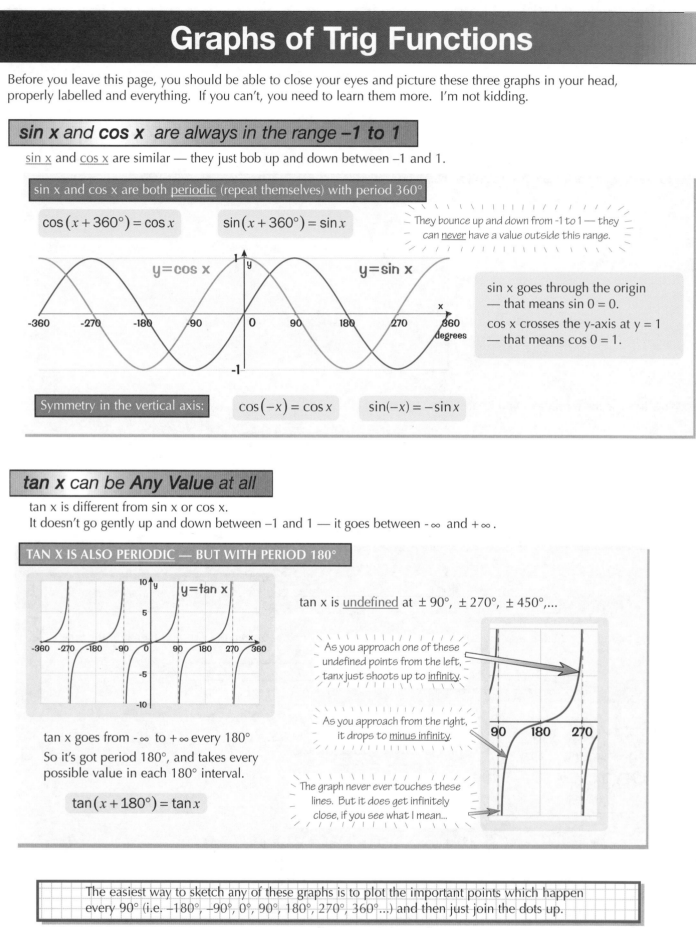

sin x and cos x are both underlined periodic (repeat themselves) with period 360°

$$\cos(x + 360°) = \cos x \qquad \sin(x + 360°) = \sin x$$

They bounce up and down from -1 to 1 — they can *never* have a value outside this range.

y=cos x   y=sin x

sin x goes through the origin — that means sin 0 = 0.
cos x crosses the y-axis at y = 1 — that means cos 0 = 1.

Symmetry in the vertical axis: $\cos(-x) = \cos x$ $\sin(-x) = -\sin x$

tan x can be *Any Value* at all

tan x is different from sin x or cos x.
It doesn't go gently up and down between –1 and 1 — it goes between $-\infty$ and $+\infty$.

TAN X IS ALSO PERIODIC — BUT WITH PERIOD 180°

y=tan x

tan x is undefined at ± 90°, ± 270°, ± 450°,...

As you approach one of these undefined points from the left, tan x just shoots up to infinity.

As you approach from the right, it drops to minus infinity.

The graph never ever touches these lines. But it does get infinitely close, if you see what I mean...

tan x goes from $-\infty$ to $+\infty$ every 180°

So it's got period 180°, and takes every possible value in each 180° interval.

$$\tan(x + 180°) = \tan x$$

The easiest way to sketch any of these graphs is to plot the important points which happen every 90° (i.e. –180°, –90°, 0°, 90°, 180°, 270°, 360°...) and then just join the dots up.

Sin and cos can make your life worthwhile — give them a chance...

It's really really really really really important that you can draw the trig graphs on this page, and get all the labels right. Make sure you know what value sin, cos and tan have at the interesting points — i.e. 0°, 90°, 180°, 270°, 360°. It's easy to remember what the graphs look like, but you've got to know exactly where they're max, min, zero, etc.

Transformed Trig Graphs

Transformed trigonometric graphs look much the same as the bog standard ones, just a little different.
There are three main types, and the changes are the same as the ones you saw on page 2 for 'normal' graphs.

There are 3 basic types of Transformed Trig Graph...

$y = n\sin x$ — a **Vertical Stretch** or **Squash**

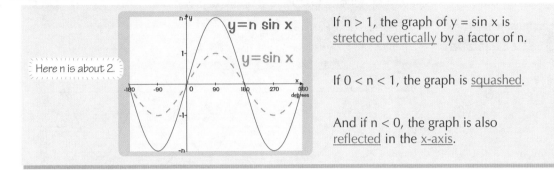

Here n is about 2.

If n > 1, the graph of y = sin x is <u>stretched vertically</u> by a factor of n.

If 0 < n < 1, the graph is <u>squashed</u>.

And if n < 0, the graph is also <u>reflected</u> in the <u>x-axis</u>.

$y = \sin nx$ — a **Horizontal Squash** or **Stretch**

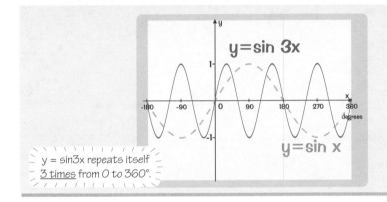

y = sin3x repeats itself
<u>3 times</u> from 0 to 360°.

If n > 1, the graph of y = sin x is <u>squashed horizontally</u> by a factor of n.

If 0 < n < 1, the graph is <u>stretched</u>.

And if n < 0, the graph is also <u>reflected</u> in the <u>y-axis</u>.

$y = \sin(x + c)$ — a **Translation** along the x-axis

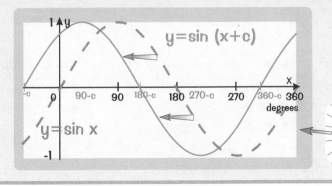

For c > 0, sin (x + c) is just sin x <u>shifted c to the left</u>.
Similarly, sin (x – c) is just sin x <u>shifted c to the right</u>.

For y = sin(x + c), the 'interesting' points are
when x + c = 0, 90°, 180°, 270°, etc.,
i.e. when x = –c, 90 – c, 180 – c, 27

Curling up on the sofa with 2cos x — that's my idea of cosi

One thing you've really got to be careful about is making sure you move or stretch the graphs in
In that last example, the graph would have moved to the right if "c" was negative. And it gets c
and vertical stretching and squashing — in the first two examples above, n > 1 means a <u>vertic</u>
<u>squash</u>. Have another look at page 2 if you're finding this confusing — it's exactly the same s

SECTION

Solving Trig Equations in a Given Interval

I used to really hate trig stuff like this. But once I'd got the hang of it, I just couldn't get enough. I stopped going out, lost interest in the opposite sex — the CAST method became my life. Learn it, but be careful. It's addictive.

There are **Two Ways** to find Solutions in an *Interval*...

> EXAMPLE: Solve $\cos x = \frac{1}{2}$ for $-360° \leq x \leq 720°$.

Like I said — there are two ways to solve this kind of question. Just use the one you prefer...

You can draw a *graph*...

Your calculator gives you a solution of 60° (but see page 5 if you didn't know this anyway). Then you have to work out what the others will be.

The other solutions are 60° either side of the graph's peaks.

1) Draw the graph of $y = \cos x$ for the range you're interested in...

2) Get the first solution from your calculator and mark this on the graph,

3) Use the symmetry of the graph to work out what the other solutions are:

$y = \cos x$

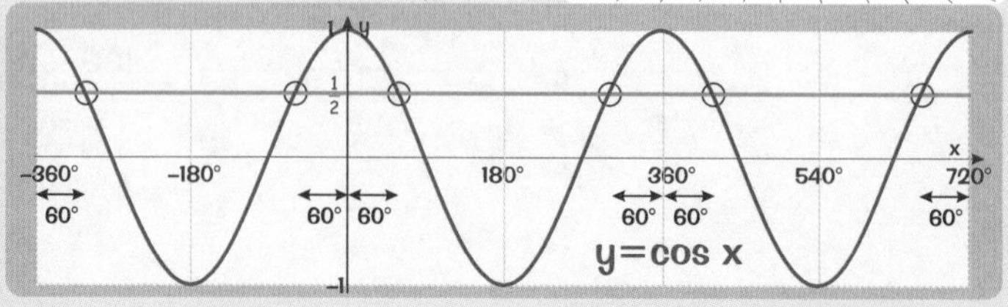

So the solutions are: $-300°, -60°, 60°, 300°, 420°$ and $660°$.

...or you can use the *CAST* diagram

CAST stands for COS, ALL, SIN, TAN — and the CAST diagram shows you where these functions are positive:

Between 90° and 180°, only SIN is positive.

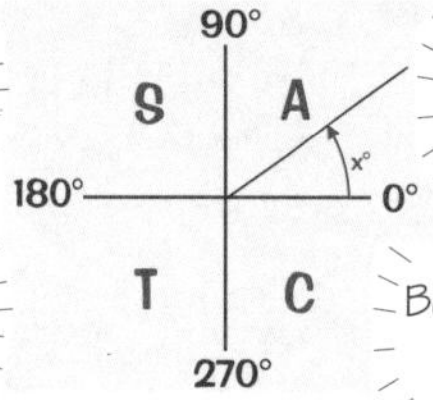

Between 0 and 90°, ALL of sin, cos and tan are positive.

Between 180° and 270°, only TAN is positive.

Between 270° and 360°, only COS is positive.

This is positive — so you're only interested in where cos is positive.

First, to find all the values of x between 0° and 360° where $\cos x = \frac{1}{2}$ — you do this:

Put the first solution onto the CAST diagram.	Find the other angles between 0° and 360° that might be solutions.	Ditch the ones that are the wrong sign.

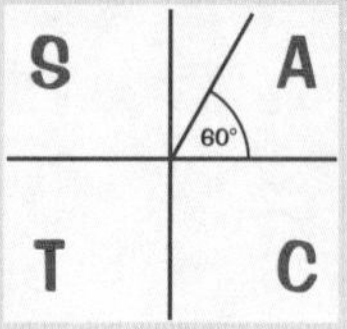

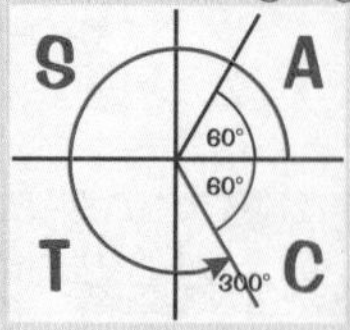

The angle from your calculator goes anticlockwise from the x-axis (unless it's negative — then it would go clockwise into the 4th quadrant).

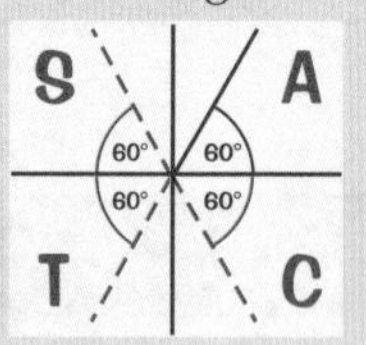

The other solutions come from making the same angle from the horizontal axis into the other 3 quadrants.

cos x = ½, which is positive. The CAST diagram tells you cos is positive in the 4th quadrant — but not the 2nd or 3rd — so ditch those two angles.

So you've got solutions 60° and 300° in the range 0° to 360°. But you need all the solutions in the range $-360°$ to $720°$. Get these by repeatedly adding or subtracting 360° onto each until you go out of range:

$$x = 60° \Rightarrow \text{(adding } 360°) \; x = 420°, 780° \text{ (too big)}$$
$$\text{and (subtracting } 360°) \; x = -300°, -660° \text{ (too small)}$$
$$x = 300° \Rightarrow \text{(adding } 360°) \; x = 660°, 1020° \text{ (too big)}$$
$$\text{and (subtracting } 360°) \; x = -60, -420° \text{ (too small)}$$

So the solutions are: $x = -300°, -60°, 60°, 300°, 420°$ and $660°$.

d I feel that love is dead, I'm loving angles instead...

e first solution you get is negative, let's say $-d°$, then you'd measure it clockwise on the CAST diagram.
the 4th quadrant. Then you'd work out the other 3 possible solutions in exactly the same way,
which weren't the right sign. Got that? No? Got that? No? Got that? Yes? Good!

Solving Trig Equations in a Given Interval

Sometimes it's a bit more complicated. But only a bit.

Sometimes you end up with sin kx = number...

For these, it's definitely easier to draw the <u>graph</u> rather than use the CAST method —
that's one reason why being able to sketch these trig graphs properly is so important.

EXAMPLE: Solve: $\sin 3x = -\frac{1}{\sqrt{2}}$ for $0° \leq x \leq 360°$.

1) You've got 3x instead of x — so when you draw the graph, make it three times as <u>squashed</u> (the period will be 120° instead of 360°).

2) When you use your calculator to get the first solution, it'll probably give you a <u>negative</u> answer (which you don't want).

$$\sin 3x = -\frac{1}{\sqrt{2}}$$
$$\Rightarrow 3x = -45°$$
$$\Rightarrow x = -15°$$

You don't want this solution — so use your graph to work out one that you do want.

This is the solution your calculator gives you...

...but these are the solutions you actually want — they're all 15° from a point where the graph crosses the x-axis.

$y = \sin 3x$

3) Using the <u>symmetry</u> of the graph, you can see that the solutions you want are:

$x = 75°, 105°, 195°, 225°, 315°$ and $345°$.

It really is mega-important that you check these answers — it's dead easy to make a silly mistake.

4) <u>Check</u> your answers by putting these values back into your calculator.

...or sin (x + k)= number

All the steps in this example are just the same as in the one above.

EXAMPLE: Solve $\sin(x + 60°) = \frac{3}{4}$ for $-360° \leq x \leq 360°$, giving your answers to 2 decimal places.

1) You've got sin (x + 60°) instead of sin x — so when you draw the graph, you have to move it 60° to the <u>left</u>.

This is the solution from the calculator.

The graph is moved 60° to the left.

$y = \sin (x+60°)$

2) Use your calculator to get that first solution...

$$\sin(x + 60°) = \frac{3}{4}$$
$$\Rightarrow x + 60° = 48.59°$$
$$\Rightarrow x = -11.41°$$

All the solutions are 48.59° from a point where the graph crosses the x-axis.

3) And again, use the graph's <u>symmetry</u> to get the other three. The solutions are:

$x = -11.41°, -288.59°, 71.41°$ and $348.59°$

4) <u>Check</u> your answers by putting these values back into your calculator.

Live a life of sin (and cos and tan)...

Yep, the examples on this page are pretty fiddly. The most important bit is actually getting the sketch right.
If you don't, you're in big trouble. Then you've just got to carefully use the sketch to work out the other solutions.
It's tricky, but you'll feel better about yourself when you've got it mastered. Ah you will, you will, you will ...

Solving Trig Equations in a Given Interval

Now for something really exciting — trig identities. Mmm, well, maybe exciting was the wrong word.
But they can be dead useful, so here goes...

For equations with **tan x** in, it often helps to use this...

$$\tan x \equiv \frac{\sin x}{\cos x}$$

This is a handy thing to know — and one the examiners love testing. Basically, if you've got a trig equation with a tan in it, together with a sin or a cos — chances are you'll be better off if you rewrite the tan using this formula.

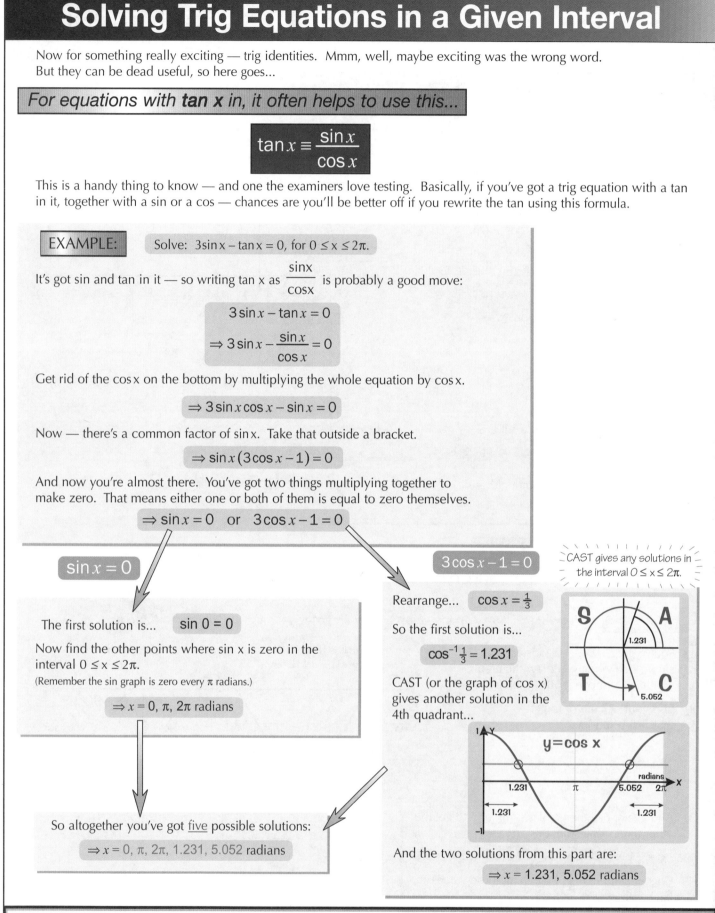

EXAMPLE: Solve: $3\sin x - \tan x = 0$, for $0 \le x \le 2\pi$.

It's got sin and tan in it — so writing tan x as $\dfrac{\sin x}{\cos x}$ is probably a good move:

$$3\sin x - \tan x = 0$$

$$\Rightarrow 3\sin x - \frac{\sin x}{\cos x} = 0$$

Get rid of the cos x on the bottom by multiplying the whole equation by cos x.

$$\Rightarrow 3\sin x \cos x - \sin x = 0$$

Now — there's a common factor of sin x. Take that outside a bracket.

$$\Rightarrow \sin x (3\cos x - 1) = 0$$

And now you're almost there. You've got two things multiplying together to make zero. That means either one or both of them is equal to zero themselves.

$$\Rightarrow \sin x = 0 \quad \text{or} \quad 3\cos x - 1 = 0$$

$\sin x = 0$

$3\cos x - 1 = 0$

CAST gives any solutions in the interval $0 \le x \le 2\pi$.

The first solution is... $\sin 0 = 0$

Now find the other points where sin x is zero in the interval $0 \le x \le 2\pi$.
(Remember the sin graph is zero every π radians.)

$$\Rightarrow x = 0, \pi, 2\pi \text{ radians}$$

Rearrange... $\cos x = \frac{1}{3}$

So the first solution is...

$$\cos^{-1}\tfrac{1}{3} = 1.231$$

CAST (or the graph of cos x) gives another solution in the 4th quadrant...

So altogether you've got <u>five</u> possible solutions:

$$\Rightarrow x = 0, \pi, 2\pi, 1.231, 5.052 \text{ radians}$$

And the two solutions from this part are:

$$\Rightarrow x = 1.231, 5.052 \text{ radians}$$

Trigonometry is the root of all evil...

What a page — you don't have fun like that every day, do you? No, trig equations are where it's at. This is a really useful trick, though — and can turn a nightmare of an equation into a bit of a pussy-cat. Rewriting stuff using different formulas is always worth trying if it feels like you're getting stuck — even if you're not sure why when you're doing it. You might have a flash of inspiration when you see the new version.

Solving Trig Equations in a Given Interval

Another trig identity — and it's a good 'un — examiners love it. And it's not difficult either.

And if you have a **sin² x** or a **cos² x**, think of this straight away...

$$\sin^2 x + \cos^2 x \equiv 1 \implies \begin{array}{l} \sin^2 x \equiv 1 - \cos^2 x \\ \cos^2 x \equiv 1 - \sin^2 x \end{array}$$

Use this identity to get rid of a sin² or a cos² that's making things awkward...

EXAMPLE: Solve: $2\sin^2 x + 5\cos x = 4$, for $0° \leq x \leq 360°$.

You can't do much while the equation's got both sin's and cos's in it. So replace the sin²x bit with 1 − cos²x.

$$2(1 - \cos^2 x) + 5\cos x = 4$$

Multiply out the bracket and rearrange it so that you've got zero on one side — and you get a quadratic in cos x:

Now the only trig function is cos.
$$\Rightarrow 2 - 2\cos^2 x + 5\cos x = 4$$
$$\Rightarrow 2\cos^2 x - 5\cos x + 2 = 0$$
If you replaced cos x with y, this would be 2y² − 5y + 2 = 0.

This is a quadratic in cos x. It's easier to factorise this if you make the substitution y = cos x.

$$2y^2 - 5y + 2 = 0$$
$$\Rightarrow (2y - 1)(y - 2) = 0$$
$$\Rightarrow (2\cos x - 1)(\cos x - 2) = 0$$
2y² − 5y + 2 = (2y ?)(y ?)
= (2y − 1)(y − 2)

Now one of the brackets must be 0. So you get 2 equations as usual:

You've already done this example on page 10.
$$(2\cos x - 1) = 0 \quad or \quad (\cos x - 2) = 0$$
This is a bit weird. cos x is always between −1 and 1. So you don't get any solutions from this bracket.

$$\cos x = \tfrac{1}{2} \Rightarrow x = 60° \quad or \quad x = 300° \quad and \quad \cos x = 2$$
This is impossible — so you get nothing from this bracket.

So at the end of all that, the only solutions you get are x = 60° and x = 300°. How boring.

Use the **Trig Identities** to prove something is the **Same** as something else

Another use for these trig identities is proving that two things are the same.

EXAMPLE: Show that $\dfrac{\cos^2 \theta}{1 + \sin \theta} \equiv 1 - \sin \theta$

The identity sign ≡ means that this is true for all θ, rather than just certain values.

Prove things like this by playing about with one side of the equation until you get the other side.

Left-hand side: $\dfrac{\cos^2 \theta}{1 + \sin \theta}$

The only thing I can think of doing here is replacing cos²θ with 1 − sin²θ. (Which is good because it works.)

$$\equiv \frac{1 - \sin^2 \theta}{1 + \sin \theta}$$
The next trick is the hardest to spot. Look at the top — does that remind you of anything?

The top line is a difference of two squares:

$$\equiv \frac{(1 + \sin \theta)(1 - \sin \theta)}{1 + \sin \theta}$$
1 − a² = (1 + a)(1 − a)
⇒ 1 − sin²θ = (1 + sinθ)(1 − sinθ)

$$\equiv 1 - \sin \theta, \underline{\text{the right-hand side.}}$$

Trig identities — the path to a brighter future...

That was a pretty miserable section. But it's over. These trig identities aren't exactly a barrel of laughs, but they are a definite source of marks — you can bet your last penny they'll be in the exam. That substitution trick to get rid of a sin² or a cos² and end up with a quadratic in sin x or cos x is a real examiners' favourite. Those identities can be a bit daunting, but it's always worth having a few tricks in the back of your mind — always look for things that factorise, or fractions that can be cancelled down, or ways to use those trig identities. Ah, it's all good clean fun.

Section Two Revision Questions

Welcome to Who wants to be a Mathematician *— the page that gives you the chance to win a million marks in your exam by answering questions on a topic of your choice. You have chosen Section Two — Trigonometry...*

For £100:   Draw a triangle ΔXYZ with sides of length x, y and z. Write down the Sine and Cosine Rules for this triangle. Write down an expression for its area.

For £200:   Write down the exact values of cos 30°, sin 30°, tan 30°, cos 45°, sin 45°, tan 45°, cos 60°, sin 60°, tan 60°. (You'll probably want to draw a couple of triangles to help you.)

For £300:   What is tan x in terms of cos and sin? What is $\cos^2 x$ in terms of $\sin^2 x$?

For £500:   Solve a) ΔABC in which A = 30°, C = 25°, b = 6m and find its area.
            b) ΔPQR in which p = 3 km, q = 23 km, R = 10°.   (answers to 2 d.p.)

For £1000:   My pet triangle Freda has sides of length 10, 20, 25. Find her angles (to 1 d.p.) and sketch her.

Well done — you now have a guaranteed win of £1000.

For £2000:   Find the 2 possible triangles ΔABC which satisfy b = 5, a = 3, A = 35°. (This is tricky: Sketch it first, and see if you can work out how to make 2 different triangles satisfying the data given.)

For £4000:   Sketch the graphs for sin x, cos x and tan x.
            Make sure you label all the max/min/zero/undefined points.

For £8000:   Sketch the following graphs:

            a) y = ½ cos 2x (for $0° \leq x \leq 360°$)   b) y = 2 sin (x+30°) (for $0° \leq x \leq 360°$)

            c) y = tan 3x (for $0° \leq x \leq 180°$)

For £16 000: Solve each of these equations for $0° \leq \theta \leq 360°$:

            a) $\sin \theta = -\frac{\sqrt{3}}{2}$ b) $\tan \theta = -1$ c) $\cos \theta = -\frac{1}{\sqrt{2}}$

For £32 000: Solve each of these equations for $-180° \leq \theta \leq 180°$ (giving your answer to 1 d.p.):

            a) $\cos 4\theta = -\frac{2}{3}$ b) $\sin(\theta + 35) = 0.3$ c) $\tan(\tfrac{1}{2}\theta) = 500$

Congratulations! You will now be taking home a cheque for at least £32000!

For £64 000: Find all the solutions to $6\sin^2 x = \cos x + 5$ in the range $0° \leq x \leq 400°$ (answers to 1 d.p.).

For £125 000: Solve 3tan x + 2 cos x = 0 for $-90° \leq x \leq 90°$

For £250 000: Simplify: $(\sin y + \cos y)^2 + (\cos y - \sin y)^2$

For £500 000: Show that $\dfrac{\sin^4 x + \sin^2 x \cos^2 x}{\cos^2 x - 1} \equiv -1$

Here comes the big one. Are you ready?

For £1 million: Which of the following identities is correct?

            A $\sin^2 x + \cos^2 x \equiv \tan^2 x$ B $\sin^2 x - \cos^2 x \equiv 1$

            C $\sin^2 ☺ + \cos^2 ♟ \equiv ♘$ D $\sin^2 x + \cos^2 x \equiv 1$

Are you sure? Is that your final answer? Perhaps you'd like to phone a teacher.

Well I can tell you, if you had said C........

.... you would have just lost £468,000...

Logs

Don't be put off by your parents or grandparents telling you that logs are hard. <u>Logarithm</u> is just a fancy word for <u>power</u>, and once you know how to use them you can solve all sorts of equations.

You need to be able to **Switch** between **Different Notations**

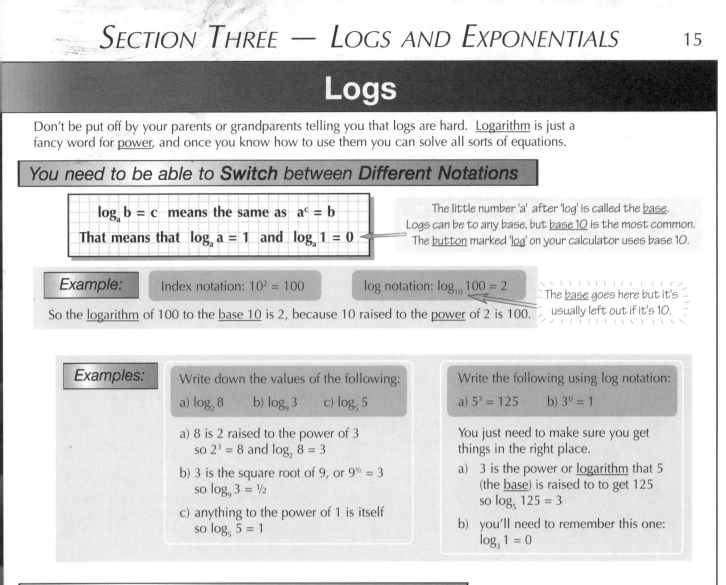

$\log_a b = c$ **means the same as** $a^c = b$

That means that $\log_a a = 1$ **and** $\log_a 1 = 0$

The little number 'a' after 'log' is called the <u>base</u>.
Logs can be to any base, but <u>base 10</u> is the most common.
The <u>button</u> marked '<u>log</u>' on your calculator uses base 10.

Example:

Index notation: $10^2 = 100$ log notation: $\log_{10} 100 = 2$

The <u>base</u> goes here but it's usually left out if it's 10.

So the <u>logarithm</u> of 100 to the <u>base 10</u> is 2, because 10 raised to the <u>power</u> of 2 is 100.

Examples:

Write down the values of the following:

a) $\log_2 8$ b) $\log_9 3$ c) $\log_5 5$

a) 8 is 2 raised to the power of 3
so $2^3 = 8$ and $\log_2 8 = 3$

b) 3 is the square root of 9, or $9^{1/2} = 3$
so $\log_9 3 = \frac{1}{2}$

c) anything to the power of 1 is itself
so $\log_5 5 = 1$

Write the following using log notation:

a) $5^3 = 125$ b) $3^0 = 1$

You just need to make sure you get things in the right place.

a)   3 is the power or <u>logarithm</u> that 5 (the <u>base</u>) is raised to to get 125
so $\log_5 125 = 3$

b)   you'll need to remember this one:
$\log_3 1 = 0$

The **Laws of Logarithms** are **Unbelievably Useful**

Whenever you have to deal with <u>logs</u>, you'll end up using the <u>laws</u> below.
That means it's no bad idea to <u>learn them</u> off by heart right now.

Laws of Logarithms

$$\log_a x + \log_a y = \log_a (xy)$$
$$\log_a x - \log_a y = \log_a \left(\frac{x}{y}\right)$$
$$\log_a x^k = k \log_a x$$

You've got to be able to change the <u>base</u> of a log too.

So $\log_7 4 = \dfrac{\log_{10} 4}{\log_{10} 7} = 0.7124$

To check: $7^{0.7124} = 4$

Change of Base

$$\log_a x = \frac{\log_b x}{\log_b a}$$

Use the **Laws** to **Manipulate Logs**

Example:

Write each expression in the form $\log_a n$, where n is a number.

a) $\log_a 5 + \log_a 4$ b) $2 \log_a 6 - \log_a 9$

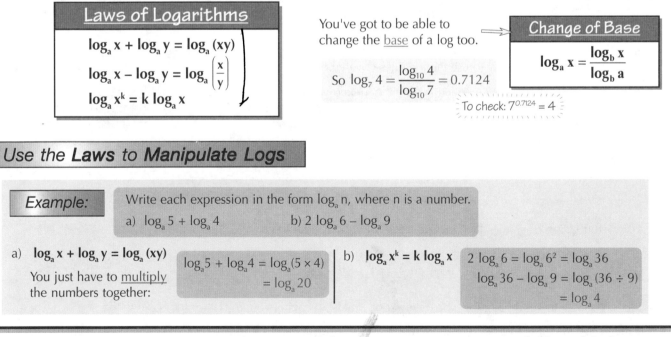

a) $\log_a x + \log_a y = \log_a (xy)$

You just have to <u>multiply</u> the numbers together:

$\log_a 5 + \log_a 4 = \log_a (5 \times 4)$
$= \log_a 20$

b) $\log_a x^k = k \log_a x$

$2 \log_a 6 = \log_a 6^2 = \log_a 36$
$\log_a 36 - \log_a 9 = \log_a (36 \div 9)$
$= \log_a 4$

It's sometimes hard to see the wood for the trees — especially with logs...

Tricky, tricky, tricky... I think of $\log_a b$ as 'the <u>power</u> I have to raise a to if I want to end up with b' — that's all it is. And the log laws make a bit more sense if you think of 'log' as meaning 'power'. For example, you know that $2^a \times 2^b = 2^{a+b}$ — this just says that if you multiply two numbers, you add the powers. Well, the first law of logs is saying the same thing. Any road up, even if you don't really understand why they work, make sure you know the log laws like you know your own navel.

Exponentials and Logs

Okay, you've done the theory of logs. So now it's a bit of stuff about exponentials (the opposite of logs, kind of), and then it'll be time to get your calculator out for a bit of button pressing...

Graphs of a^x Never Reach Zero

All the graphs of $y = a^x$ (exponential graphs) where $a > 1$ have the same basic shape. The graphs for $a = 2$, $a = 3$ and $a = 4$ are shown on the right.

- All the a's are greater than 1 — so y increases as x increases.
- The bigger a is, the quicker the graphs increase. The rate at which they increase gets bigger too.
- As x decreases, y decreases at a smaller and smaller rate — y will approach zero, but never actually get there.

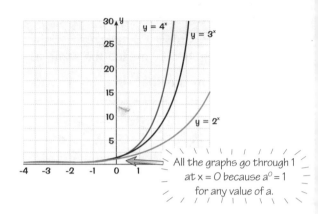

All the graphs go through 1 at $x = 0$ because $a^0 = 1$ for any value of a.

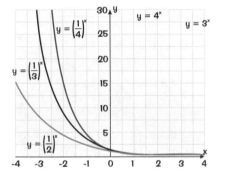

The graphs on the left are for $y = a^x$ where $a < 1$ (they're for $a = \frac{1}{2}, \frac{1}{3}$ and $\frac{1}{4}$).

- All the a's are less than 1 — meaning y decreases as x increases.
- As x increases, y decreases at a smaller and smaller rate — again, y will approach zero, but never actually get there.
- In fact, they're reflections in the y-axis of the graphs above.

  If you think about it, this is what you'd expect, since they show $y = a^{-x}$ for $a = 2$, 3, and 4 — i.e. they're transformations of the form $y = f(-x)$, like the ones described on page 2.

Use the Calculator Log Button Whenever You Can

Example: Use logarithms to solve the following for x, giving the answers to 4 s.f.

a) $10^x = 170$ b) $10^{3x} = 4000$ c) $7^x = 55$ d) $\log_{10} x = 1.8$ e) $\log_2 x = 5$

You've got the magic buttons on your calculator, but you'd better follow the instructions and show that you know how to use the log rules covered earlier.

a) $10^x = 170$ — when you get an equation with the 'unknown' in the power, take logs of both sides of the equation (which you do by writing 'log' in front of both sides). Then you can use the laws of logs to fiddle about with the result. In theory, it doesn't matter what base you use, but your calculator has a '$\log_{10}$' button, so base 10 is usually a good idea. But whatever base you use, use the same one for both sides.

So taking logs to base 10 of both sides of the above equation gives: $\log 10^x = \log 170$

i.e. $x \log 10 = \log 170$ ⟵ Since $\log_{10} 10 = 1$.

i.e. $x = \log 170 = 2.230$ (to 4 sig. fig)

b) $10^{3x} = 4000$. Same again — take logs (to base 10) of both sides to get: $3x = \log_{10} 4000 = 3.602$, so $x = 1.201$

c) $7^x = 55$. Once again, take logs of both sides, and use the log rules: $x \log_{10} 7 = \log_{10} 55$, so $x = \dfrac{\log_{10} 55}{\log_{10} 7} = 2.059$

d) $\log_{10} x = 1.8$ — to get rid of a log, you 'take exponentials', meaning you do '10 (or the base) to the power of each side'.

Think of 'taking logs' and 'taking exponentials' as opposite processes — one cancels the other out: $10^{\log_{10} x} = 10^{1.8}$

Or you can simply use the formula on p15 — whichever you prefer

i.e. $x = 63.10$

e) $\log_2 x = 5$. Here, the base is 2, so 'taking exponentials' means doing '2 to the power of both sides': $2^{\log_2 x} = 2^5$

i.e. $x = 2^5 = 32$

Section Three Revision Questions

Logs* and exponentials are surprisingly useful things. As well as being in your exam they pop up all over the place in real life — savings, radioactive decay, growth of bacteria — all log*arithmic.

And now for something (marginally) different:

1) Write down the values of the following:
   a) $\log_3 27$
   b) $\log_3 (1 \div 27)$
   c) $\log_3 18 - \log_3 2$

2) Simplify the following:
   a) $\log 3 + 2 \log 5$
   b) $\frac{1}{2} \log 36 - \log 3$

3) Simplify $\log_b (\chi^2 - 1) - \log_b (\chi - 1)$

4) Copy and complete the table for the function $y = 4^x$:

x	−3	−2	−1	0	1	2	3
y							

   a) Using suitable scales, plot a graph of $y = 4^x$ for $-3 < x < 3$.
   b) Use the graph to solve the equation $4^x = 20$.

5) Solve these little jokers:
   a) $10^x = 240$
   b) $\log_{10} x = 2.6$
   c) $10^{2x+1} = 1500$
   d) $4^{(x-1)} = 200$

6) Find the smallest integer P such that $1.5^P > 1\,000\,000$

*   *He's a lumberjack and he's okay.*
     He sleeps all night and he works all day.

Sequences

A sequence is a list of numbers that follow a <u>certain pattern</u>. Sequences can be <u>finite</u> or <u>infinite</u> (infinity — oooh), and they're usually generated in one of two ways. And guess what? You have to know everything about them.

A **Sequence** can be defined by its nth **Term**

You may well have covered this stuff at GCSE — if so, you've got <u>no excuses</u> for mucking it up.

With some sequences, you can work out any <u>value</u> (the nth term) from its <u>position</u> in the sequence (<u>n</u>). And often, you can even work out a <u>formula</u> for the nth term.

> **Example:**   Find the nth term of the sequence 5, 8, 11, 14, 17, ...
>
> | 1st | 2nd | 3rd | 4th | 5th |
> |------|------|------|------|------|
> | 5 | 8 | 11 | 14 | 17 |
>
> +3   +3   +3   +3
>
> Each term is <u>3 more</u> than the one before it. That means that you need to start by <u>multiplying n by 3</u>.
>
> Take the first term (where n = 1). If you multiply n by 3, you still have to <u>add 2</u> to get 5.
>
> The same goes for n = 2. To get 8 you need to multiply n by 3, then add 2.
> Every term in the sequence is worked out exactly the same way.
>
> So the nth term is $3n + 2$

You can define a sequence by a **Recurrence Relation** too

Don't be put off by the fancy name — recurrence relations are pretty <u>easy</u> really.

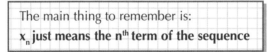

> The main thing to remember is:
> x_n **just means the nth term of the sequence**

The <u>next term</u> in the sequence is x_{n+1}. You need to describe how to <u>work out</u> x_{n+1} if you're given x_n.
What you're actually doing is working out x_{n+1} as a <u>function</u> of x_n, so you can write $x_{n+1} = f(x_n)$.

> **Example:**   Find the recurrence relation of the sequence 5, 8, 11, 14, 17, ...
>
> From the example above, you know that each term equals the one before it, plus 3.
>
> This is written like this: $x_{n+1} = x_n + 3$
>
> In everyday language, $x_{n+1} = x_n + 3$ means that the second term equals the first term plus 3.
>
> <u>BUT</u> $x_{n+1} = x_n + 3$ on its own <u>isn't enough</u> to describe 5, 8, 11, 14, 17,...
> For example, the sequence 87, 90, 93, 96, 99, ... <u>also</u> has each term being 3 more than the one before.
>
> The recurrence relation needs to be more <u>specific</u>, so you've got to <u>give one term</u> in the sequence.
> You almost always give the <u>first value</u>, x_1.
>
> Putting all of this together gives 5, 8, 11, 14, 17,... as $x_{n+1} = x_n + 3$, $x_1 = 5$

Like maths teachers, sequences can go on and on and on and on...

If you know the formula for the nth term, you can work out any term using a single formula, so it's kind of easy. If you only know a recurrence relation, then you can only work out the <u>next</u> term. So if you want the 20th term, and you only know the first one, then you have to use the recurrence relation 19 times. (So it'd be quicker to work out a formula really.)

Sequences

Some sequences involve **Multiplying**

You've done the easy 'adding' business. Now it gets really tough — <u>multiplying</u>. Are you sure you're ready for this...

Example: A sequence is defined by $x_{n+1} = 2x_n - 1$, $x_2 = 5$. List the first five terms.

OK, you're told the second term, $x_2 = 5$. Just <u>plug that value</u> into the equation, and carry on from there.

$x_3 = 2 \times 5 - 1 = 9$ ⟵ From the equation $x_n = x_2$ so $x_{n+1} = x_3$

$x_4 = 2 \times 9 - 1 = 17$ ⟵

$x_5 = 2 \times 17 - 1 = 33$ ⟵ Now use x_3 to find $x_{n+1} = x_4$ and so on...

Now to find the first term, a_1:

$x_2 = 2x_1 - 1$ ⟵ Just make $x_n = x_1$

$5 = 2x_1 - 1$

$2x_1 = 6$

$x_1 = 3$

So the first five terms of the sequence are $3, 5, 9, 17, 33$.

Some Sequences have a **Certain Number** of terms — others go on **Forever**

Some sequences are only defined for a <u>certain number</u> of terms.

For example, $x_{n+1} = x_n + 3$, $x_1 = 1$, $1 \le n \le 20$ will be 1, 4, 7, 10, ..., 58 and will contain 20 terms.
This is a finite sequence.

Other sequences <u>don't</u> have a specified number of terms and could go on <u>forever</u>.

For example, $u_{k+1} = u_k + 2$, $u_1 = 5$, will be 5, 7, 9, 11, 13, ... and won't have a final term.
This is an infinite sequence.

While others are <u>periodic</u>, and just revisit the same values over and over again.

For example, $u_k = u_{k-3}$, $u_1 = 1$, $u_2 = 4$, $u_3 = 2$, will be 1, 4, 2, 1, 4, 2, 1, 4, 2,...
This is a periodic sequence with period 3.

You can use **Recurrence Relations** to find the **Limit** of a sequence

Some sequences <u>tend to a limit</u> — the terms get <u>closer and closer</u> to a certain number (but don't necessarily ever reach it).

Example: A sequence has the recurrence relation $x_{n+1} = \frac{1}{2}x_n + 1$, and $x_1 = 1$.

So the terms of this sequence are: $x_1 = 1$, $x_2 = 1.5$, $x_3 = 1.75$, $x_4 = 1.875$, $x_5 = 1.9375$, $x_6 = 1.96875$, $x_7 = 1.984375$, etc.

1) The terms are getting closer and closer to 2.
 And even though no term will ever actually be equal to 2, the limit of the sequence is still 2.

2) This is written: $x_n \to 2$ as $n \to \infty$, and you say, "x_n *tends to 2 as n tends to infinity*."

Not all sequences tend to a limit as $n \to \infty$ (e.g. the sequence 1, 2, 3, 4, 5... just gets bigger and bigger as $n \to \infty$).
But if a sequence does tend to a limit, you can find it by using the <u>recurrence relation</u>.

$$x_{n+1} = f(x_n)$$

Once the sequence reaches its limit (which it might not do until $x = \infty$), it <u>stays there</u>.
So to find the limit (often called L), you solve <u>L = f(L)</u>.

The recurrence relation
was $x_{n+1} = \frac{1}{2}x_n + 1$.

Example: To find the limit of the above sequence, you solve: <u>$L = \frac{1}{2}L + 1$</u>. ⟵
 i.e. $L - \frac{1}{2}L = 1$
 i.e. $\frac{1}{2}L = 1$, and so <u>$L = 2$</u>, meaning the limit of the sequence is 2.

Arithmetic Progressions

Right, you've got basic sequences tucked under your belt now — time to step it up a notch (sounds painful).
When the terms of a sequence progress by <u>adding</u> a <u>fixed amount</u> each time, this is called an <u>arithmetic progression</u>.

It's all about *Finding* the nth *Term*

The <u>first term</u> of a sequence is given the symbol **a**. The <u>amount you add</u> each time is the common difference, called **d**.
The <u>position of any term</u> in the sequence is called **n**.

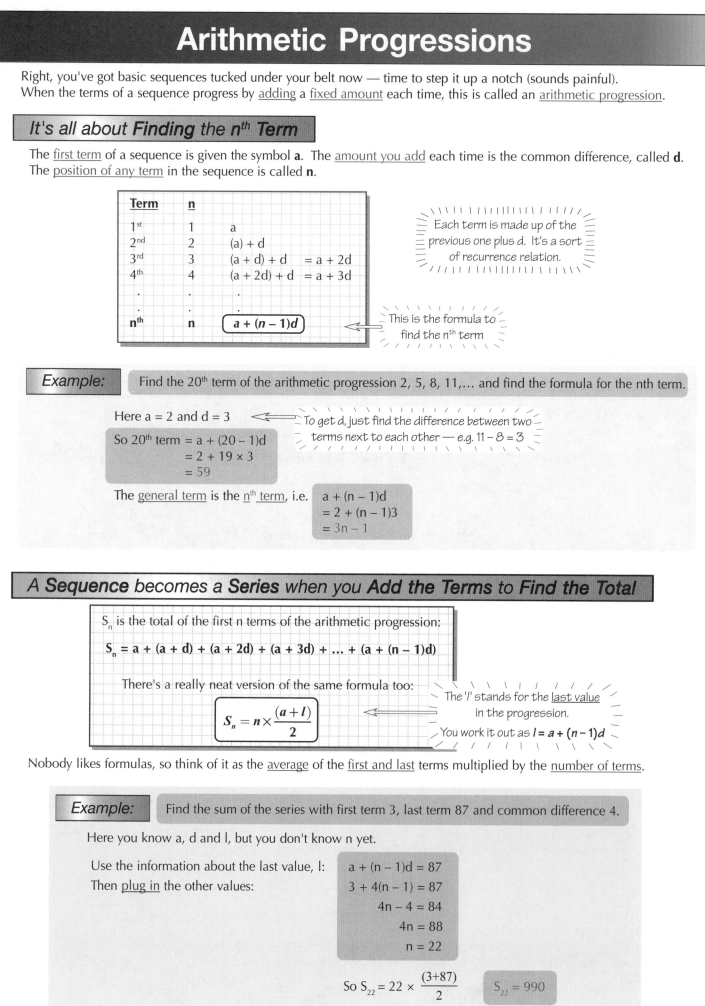

Term	n	
1st	1	a
2nd	2	(a) + d
3rd	3	(a + d) + d = a + 2d
4th	4	(a + 2d) + d = a + 3d
.	.	.
.	.	.
n^{th}	n	$a + (n - 1)d$

Each term is made up of the previous one plus d. It's a sort of recurrence relation.

This is the formula to find the nth term

Example: Find the 20th term of the arithmetic progression 2, 5, 8, 11,… and find the formula for the nth term.

Here a = 2 and d = 3

To get d, just find the difference between two terms next to each other — e.g. 11 – 8 = 3

So 20th term $= a + (20 - 1)d$
$= 2 + 19 \times 3$
$= 59$

The <u>general term</u> is the nth <u>term</u>, i.e. $a + (n - 1)d$
$= 2 + (n - 1)3$
$= 3n - 1$

A *Sequence* becomes a *Series* when you *Add the Terms* to *Find the Total*

S_n is the total of the first n terms of the arithmetic progression:

$$S_n = a + (a + d) + (a + 2d) + (a + 3d) + \ldots + (a + (n - 1)d)$$

There's a really neat version of the same formula too:

$$S_n = n \times \frac{(a+l)}{2}$$

The 'l' stands for the <u>last value</u> in the progression.
You work it out as $l = a + (n - 1)d$

Nobody likes formulas, so think of it as the <u>average</u> of the <u>first and last</u> terms multiplied by the <u>number of terms</u>.

Example: Find the sum of the series with first term 3, last term 87 and common difference 4.

Here you know a, d and l, but you don't know n yet.

Use the information about the last value, l:
Then <u>plug in</u> the other values:

$a + (n - 1)d = 87$
$3 + 4(n - 1) = 87$
$4n - 4 = 84$
$4n = 88$
$n = 22$

So $S_{22} = 22 \times \frac{(3+87)}{2}$ $S_{22} = 990$

Arithmetic Progressions

It's not always that simple though.
Should've done English, should've done English, should've done English, should've done English, should've done English...

They **Won't** always give you the **Last Term**...

...but don't panic — there's a formula to use when the last term is unknown. But you knew I'd say that, didn't you?

You know $l = a + (n - 1)d$ and $S_n = n\dfrac{(a+l)}{2}$.

Plug l into S_n and rearrange to get the formula in the box:

$$S_n = \frac{n}{2}[2a + (n-1)d]$$

Example: For the sequence -5, -2, 1, 4, 7, ... find the sum of the first 20 terms.

So a = -5 and d = 3. The question says n = 20 too.

$$S_{20} = \frac{20}{2}[2\times-5+(20-1)\times3]$$
$$= 10\,[-10+19\times3]$$
$$S_{20} = 470$$

There's **Another** way of **Writing Series**, too

So far, the letter S has been used for the sum. The Greeks did a lot of work on this — their capital letter for S is sigma, or Σ. This is used today, together with the general term, to mean the sum of the series.

Example:

...and ending with n=15

Find $\displaystyle\sum_{n=1}^{15}(2n+3)$

Starting with n=1...

This means you have to find the sum of the first 15 terms of the series with n^{th} term 2n + 3.

The first term ($n = 1$) is 5, the second term ($n = 2$) is 7, the third is 9, ... and the last term ($n = 15$) is 33. In other words, you need to find 5 + 7 + 9 + ... + 33. This gives $a = 5$, $d = 2$, $n = 15$ and $l = 33$.

You know all of a, d, n and l, so you can use either formula:

$$S_n = n\frac{(a+l)}{2}$$
$$S_{15} = 15\frac{(5+33)}{2}$$
$$S_{15} = 15 \times 19$$
$$S_{15} = 285$$

It makes no difference which method you use.

$$S_n = \frac{n}{2}[2a + (n-1)d]$$
$$S_{15} = \frac{15}{2}[2\times5 + 14\times2]$$
$$S_{15} = \frac{15}{2}[10+28]$$
$$S_{15} = 285$$

This sigma notation is all Greek to me... (Ho ho ho)

A sequence is just a list of numbers (with commas between them) — a series on the other hand is when you add all the terms together. It doesn't sound like a big difference, but mathematicians get all hot under the collar when you get the two mixed up. Remember that BlackADDer was a great TV series — not a TV sequence. (Sounds daft, but I bet you remember it n

Arithmetic Progressions

Use *Arithmetic Progressions* to add up the *First n Whole Numbers*

The <u>sum of the first n natural numbers</u> looks like this: $S_n = 1 + 2 + 3 + \ldots + (n-2) + (n-1) + n$

So a = 1, l = n and also n = n. Now just plug those values into the formula:

$$S_n = n \times \frac{(a+l)}{2} \implies \boxed{S_n = \frac{1}{2}n(n+1)}$$

<u>Natural numbers</u> are just positive whole numbers.

Example: Add up all the whole numbers from 1 to 100.

Sounds pretty hard, but all you have to do is stick it into the formula:

$S_{100} = \frac{1}{2} \times 100 \times 101$. So $S_{100} = 5050$

Series *Don't* have to start with *n = 1*

Instead of adding up numbers from 1 to 100, you can add the natural numbers from, say, 50 to 100. This just means the sum from 1 to 100, but <u>without</u> the first 49 whole numbers.

You can write this as
$$\sum_{n=50}^{100} n = \sum_{n=1}^{100} n - \sum_{n=1}^{49} n$$

Using $S_n = \frac{n(n+1)}{2}$

$$= 5050 - \frac{49 \times 50}{2}$$

From the example above.

$$= 5050 - 1225$$
$$= 3825$$

Subtract any *Series* if it *Doesn't* Start at *n = 1*

Example: Find $\displaystyle\sum_{n=7}^{20}(4n-1)$

$$\sum_{n=7}^{20}(4n-1) = \sum_{n=1}^{20}(4n-1) - \sum_{n=1}^{6}(4n-1)$$

Using $S_n = n\frac{(a+l)}{2}$

$$= \frac{20(3+79)}{2} - \frac{6(3+23)}{2}$$
$$= 820 - 78$$
$$= 742$$

NB: $\displaystyle\sum_{n=1}^{20}(4n-1)$ and $\displaystyle\sum_{n=1}^{6}(4n-1)$ could both have been worked out a different way:

$$\sum_{n=1}^{6}(4n-1) = \sum_{n=1}^{6}4n - \sum_{n=1}^{6}1$$

$$= 4\sum_{n=1}^{6}n - \sum_{n=1}^{6}1$$

Because $\displaystyle\sum_{n=1}^{6}4n = 4\sum_{n=1}^{6}n$

$\displaystyle\sum_{n=1}^{6}1 = 1+1+1+1+1+1 = 6$

$$= 4\left(\frac{6 \times 7}{2}\right) - 6$$
$$= 78$$

Geometric Progressions

So <u>arithmetic progressions</u> mean you <u>add</u> a number to get the next term.
<u>Geometric progressions</u> are a bit different — you <u>multiply</u> by a number to get the next term.

Geometric Progressions Multiply by a Constant each time

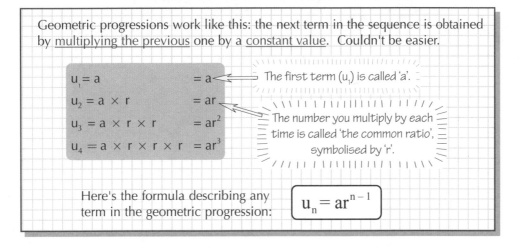

Geometric progressions work like this: the next term in the sequence is obtained by <u>multiplying the previous</u> one by a <u>constant value</u>. Couldn't be easier.

$$u_1 = a \qquad\qquad = a$$
$$u_2 = a \times r \qquad\quad = ar$$
$$u_3 = a \times r \times r \qquad = ar^2$$
$$u_4 = a \times r \times r \times r = ar^3$$

The first term (u_1) is called 'a'.

The number you multiply by each time is called 'the common ratio', symbolised by 'r'.

Here's the formula describing any term in the geometric progression: $\boxed{u_n = ar^{n-1}}$

Example:

There is a chessboard with a 1p piece on the first square, 2p on the second square, 4p on the third, 8p on the fourth and so on until the board is full. Calculate <u>how much money</u> is on the board.

This is a <u>geometric progression</u>, where you get the next term in the sequence by multiplying the previous one by 2.
So a = 1 (because you start with 1p on the first square) and r = 2.

So $u_1 = 1, u_2 = 2, u_3 = 4, u_4 = 8, ...$

You often have to work out the Sum of the Terms

Just like before, S_n stands for the <u>sum</u> of the <u>first n terms</u>.
In the example above, you're told to work out S_{64} (because there are 64 squares on a chessboard).

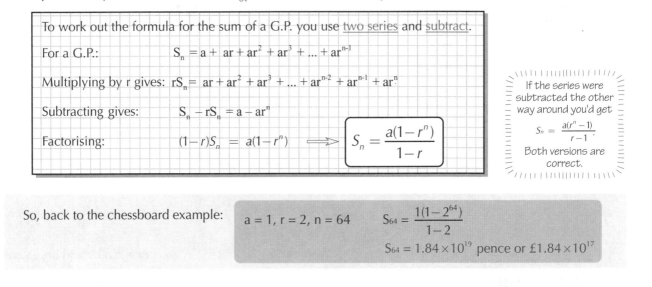

To work out the formula for the sum of a G.P. you use <u>two series</u> and <u>subtract</u>.

For a G.P.: $\qquad\qquad\qquad S_n = a + ar + ar^2 + ar^3 + ... + ar^{n-1}$

Multiplying by r gives: $\quad rS_n = ar + ar^2 + ar^3 + ... + ar^{n-2} + ar^{n-1} + ar^n$

Subtracting gives: $\qquad\quad S_n - rS_n = a - ar^n$

Factorising: $\qquad\qquad (1-r)S_n = a(1-r^n) \implies \boxed{S_n = \dfrac{a(1-r^n)}{1-r}}$

If the series were subtracted the other way around you'd get
$$S_n = \frac{a(r^n - 1)}{r - 1}.$$
Both versions are correct.

So, back to the chessboard example: $\quad a = 1, r = 2, n = 64 \qquad S_{64} = \dfrac{1(1 - 2^{64})}{1 - 2}$

$$S_{64} = 1.84 \times 10^{19} \text{ pence or } £1.84 \times 10^{17}$$

The whole is more than the sum of the parts — hmm, not in maths, it ain't...

You really need to understand the difference between arithmetic and geometric progressions — it's not hard, but it needs to be fixed firmly in your head. There are only a few formulas for sequences and series (the nth term of a sequence, the sum of the first n terms of a series), but you need to learn them, since they won't be in the formula book they give you.

Geometric Progressions

Geometric progressions can either *Grow* or *Shrink*

In the chessboard example, each term was <u>bigger</u> than the previous one, 1, 2, 4, 8, 16, …
You can create a series where each term is <u>less</u> than the previous one by using a <u>small value of r</u>.

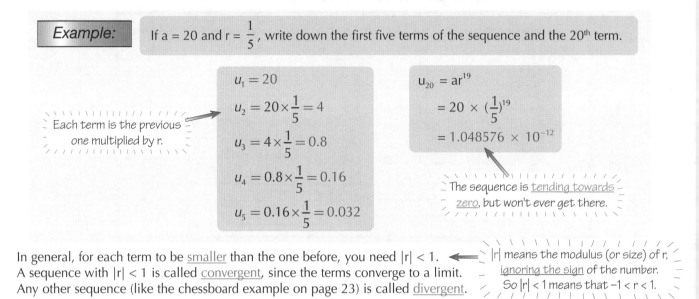

Example: If $a = 20$ and $r = \dfrac{1}{5}$, write down the first five terms of the sequence and the 20th term.

$u_1 = 20$

$u_2 = 20 \times \dfrac{1}{5} = 4$

$u_3 = 4 \times \dfrac{1}{5} = 0.8$

$u_4 = 0.8 \times \dfrac{1}{5} = 0.16$

$u_5 = 0.16 \times \dfrac{1}{5} = 0.032$

Each term is the previous one multiplied by r.

$u_{20} = ar^{19}$

$= 20 \times \left(\dfrac{1}{5}\right)^{19}$

$= 1.048576 \times 10^{-12}$

The sequence is <u>tending towards zero</u>, but won't ever get there.

In general, for each term to be <u>smaller</u> than the one before, you need $|r| < 1$.
A sequence with $|r| < 1$ is called <u>convergent</u>, since the terms converge to a limit.
Any other sequence (like the chessboard example on page 23) is called <u>divergent</u>.

$|r|$ means the modulus (or size) of r, <u>ignoring the sign</u> of the number. So $|r| < 1$ means that $-1 < r < 1$.

A *Convergent* series has a *Sum* to *Infinity*

In other words, if you just <u>kept</u> adding terms to a <u>convergent</u> series, you'd get <u>closer and closer</u> to a certain number, but you'd never actually reach it.

If $|r| < 1$ and n is very, very <u>big</u>, then r^n will be very, very <u>small</u> — or to put it technically, $r^n \to 0$. (Try working out $(1/2)^{100}$ on your calculator if you don't believe me.)

This means $(1 - r^n)$ is really, really close to 1.

So, as $n \to \infty$, $S_n \to \dfrac{a}{1-r}$.

It's easier to remember as $\boxed{S_\infty = \dfrac{a}{1-r}}$

S_∞ just means 'sum to infinity'.

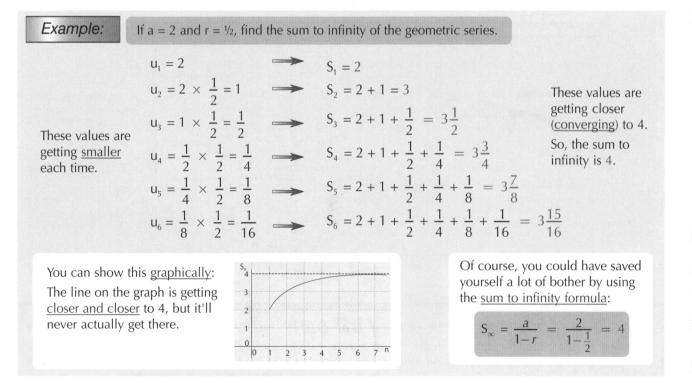

Example: If $a = 2$ and $r = \frac{1}{2}$, find the sum to infinity of the geometric series.

These values are getting <u>smaller</u> each time.

$u_1 = 2$

$u_2 = 2 \times \dfrac{1}{2} = 1$

$u_3 = 1 \times \dfrac{1}{2} = \dfrac{1}{2}$

$u_4 = \dfrac{1}{2} \times \dfrac{1}{2} = \dfrac{1}{4}$

$u_5 = \dfrac{1}{4} \times \dfrac{1}{2} = \dfrac{1}{8}$

$u_6 = \dfrac{1}{8} \times \dfrac{1}{2} = \dfrac{1}{16}$

$S_1 = 2$

$S_2 = 2 + 1 = 3$

$S_3 = 2 + 1 + \dfrac{1}{2} = 3\dfrac{1}{2}$

$S_4 = 2 + 1 + \dfrac{1}{2} + \dfrac{1}{4} = 3\dfrac{3}{4}$

$S_5 = 2 + 1 + \dfrac{1}{2} + \dfrac{1}{4} + \dfrac{1}{8} = 3\dfrac{7}{8}$

$S_6 = 2 + 1 + \dfrac{1}{2} + \dfrac{1}{4} + \dfrac{1}{8} + \dfrac{1}{16} = 3\dfrac{15}{16}$

These values are getting closer (converging) to 4.
So, the sum to infinity is 4.

You can show this <u>graphically</u>:
The line on the graph is getting <u>closer and closer</u> to 4, but it'll never actually get there.

Of course, you could have saved yourself a lot of bother by using the <u>sum to infinity formula</u>:

$S_\infty = \dfrac{a}{1-r} = \dfrac{2}{1 - \dfrac{1}{2}} = 4$

Geometric Progressions

A *Divergent* series *Doesn't* have a sum to infinity

Example: If $a = 2$ and $r = 2$, find the sum to infinity of the series.

$$u_1 = 2 \implies S_1 = 2$$
$$u_2 = 2 \times 2 = 4 \implies S_2 = 2 + 4 = 6$$
$$u_3 = 4 \times 2 = 8 \implies S_3 = 2 + 4 + 8 = 14$$
$$u_4 = 8 \times 2 = 16 \implies S_4 = 2 + 4 + 8 + 16 = 30$$
$$u_5 = 16 \times 2 = 32 \implies S_5 = 2 + 4 + 8 + 16 + 32 = 62$$

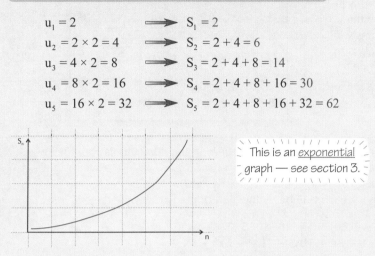

This is an <u>exponential</u> graph — see section 3.

As $n \to \infty$, $S_n \to \infty$ in a big way. So big, in fact, that eventually you <u>can't work it out</u> — so don't bother.

There is <u>no sum to infinity</u> for a <u>divergent</u> series.

Example: When a baby is born, £3000 is invested in an account with a fixed interest rate of 4% per year.
a) What will the account be worth at the start of the seventh year?
b) Will the account have doubled in value by the time the child reaches its 21st birthday?

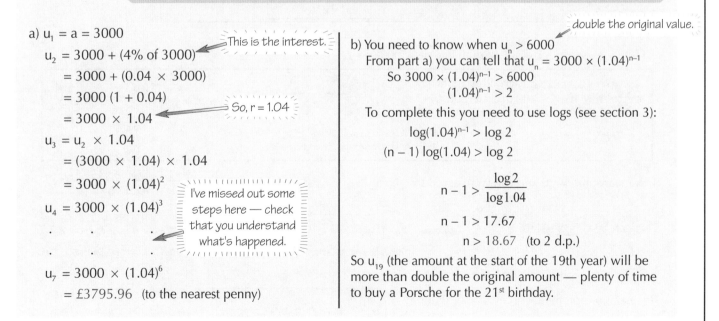

a) $u_1 = a = 3000$

$u_2 = 3000 + (4\% \text{ of } 3000)$ ← This is the interest.

$\quad = 3000 + (0.04 \times 3000)$

$\quad = 3000 (1 + 0.04)$

$\quad = 3000 \times 1.04$ ← So, r = 1.04

$u_3 = u_2 \times 1.04$

$\quad = (3000 \times 1.04) \times 1.04$

$\quad = 3000 \times (1.04)^2$

$u_4 = 3000 \times (1.04)^3$

I've missed out some steps here — check that you understand what's happened.

$\quad \cdot \quad \cdot \quad \cdot$
$\quad \cdot \quad \cdot \quad \cdot$

$u_7 = 3000 \times (1.04)^6$

$\quad = £3795.96$ (to the nearest penny)

b) You need to know when $u_n > 6000$ — double the original value.
From part a) you can tell that $u_n = 3000 \times (1.04)^{n-1}$
So $3000 \times (1.04)^{n-1} > 6000$
$\quad (1.04)^{n-1} > 2$

To complete this you need to use logs (see section 3):
$$\log(1.04)^{n-1} > \log 2$$
$$(n - 1) \log(1.04) > \log 2$$
$$n - 1 > \frac{\log 2}{\log 1.04}$$
$$n - 1 > 17.67$$
$$n > 18.67 \quad \text{(to 2 d.p.)}$$

So u_{19} (the amount at the start of the 19th year) will be more than double the original amount — plenty of time to buy a Porsche for the 21st birthday.

So tell me — if my savings earn 4% per year, when will I be rich...

Now here's a funny thing — you can have a convergent geometric series if the common ratio is small enough.
I find this odd — that I can keep adding things to a sum forever, but the sum never gets really really big.

Binomial Expansions

If you're feeling a bit stressed, just take a couple of minutes to relax before trying to get your head round this page — it's a bit of a stinker in places. Have a cup of tea and think about something else for a couple of minutes. Ready...

Writing *Binomial Expansions* is all about *Spotting Patterns*

Doing binomial expansions just involves <u>multiplying out</u> the brackets. It would get nasty when you raise the brackets to <u>higher powers</u> — but once again I've got a <u>cunning plan</u>...

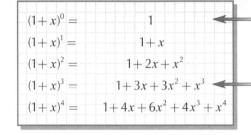

$$(1+x)^0 = 1$$
$$(1+x)^1 = 1+x$$
$$(1+x)^2 = 1+2x+x^2$$
$$(1+x)^3 = 1+3x+3x^2+x^3$$
$$(1+x)^4 = 1+4x+6x^2+4x^3+x^4$$

Anything to the power 0 is 1.

$$(1+x)^3 = (1+x)(1+x)^2$$
$$= (1+x)(1+2x+x^2)$$
$$= 1+2x+x^2+x+2x^2+x^3$$
$$= 1+3x+3x^2+x^3$$

A Frenchman named Pascal spotted the pattern in the coefficients and wrote them down in a <u>triangle</u>.
So it was called 'Pascal's Triangle' (imaginative, eh?).
The pattern's easy — each number is the <u>sum</u> of the two above it.

So, the next line will be: **1 5 10 10 5 1**
giving **(1 + x)⁵ = 1 + 5x + 10x² + 10x³ + 5x⁴ + x⁵.**

```
            1
          1   1
        1   2   1
      1   3   3 + 1
    1   4   6  = 4   1
```

You *Don't* need to write out Pascal's Triangle for *Higher Powers*

There's a formula for the numbers in the triangle. The formula looks <u>horrible</u> (one of the worst in AS maths) so don't try to learn it letter by letter — look for the <u>patterns</u> in it instead. Here's an example:

Example: Expand $(1 + x)^{20}$, giving the first four terms only.

So you can use this formula for any power, the power is called n. In this example n = 20.

$$(1+x)^n = 1 + \frac{n}{1}x + \frac{n(n-1)}{1\times2}x^2 + \boxed{\frac{n(n-1)(n-2)}{1\times2\times3}x^3} + \ldots\ldots + x^n$$

Here's a closer look at the term in the black box:

There are <u>three things</u> multiplied together on the top row. If n=20, this would be 20×19×18.

$$\frac{n(n-1)(n-2)}{1\times2\times3}x^3$$

<u>Start here</u>. The power of x is 3 and everything else here is based on 3.

There are <u>three integers</u> here multiplied together.
1×2×3 is written as 3! and called 3 <u>factorial</u>.

This means, if n = 20 and you were asked for '<u>the term in x⁷</u>' you should write $\frac{20\times19\times18\times17\times16\times15\times14}{1\times2\times3\times4\times5\times6\times7}x^7$.

This can be <u>simplified</u> to $\frac{20!}{7!13!}x^7$ ← $20\times19\times18\times17\times16\times15\times14 = \frac{20!}{13!}$ because it's the numbers from 20 to 1 multiplied together, divided by the numbers from 13 to 1 multiplied together.

Believe it or not, there's an even <u>shorter</u> form: $\frac{20!}{7!13!}$ is written as $^{20}C_7$ or $\binom{20}{7}$

$$^nC_r = \binom{n}{r} = \frac{n!}{r!(n-r)!}$$

So, to finish the example, $(1+x)^{20} = 1 + \frac{20}{1}x + \frac{20\times19}{1\times2}x^2 + \frac{20\times19\times18}{1\times2\times3}x^3 + \ldots = 1 + 20x + 190x^2 + 1140x^3 + \ldots$

Binomial Expansions

It's slightly more complicated when the Coefficient of x isn't 1

Example: What is the term in x^5 in the expansion of $(1 - 3x)^{12}$?

The term in x^5 will be as follows:

$$\frac{12 \times 11 \times 10 \times 9 \times 8}{1 \times 2 \times 3 \times 4 \times 5}(-3x)^5$$

Watch out — the –3 is included here with the x.

$$= \frac{12!}{5!7!}(-3)^5 x^5 \quad = -\frac{12!}{5!7!} \times 3^5 x^5 = -192456x^5$$

Note that $(-3)^{even}$ will always be <u>positive</u> and $(-3)^{odd}$ will always be <u>negative</u>.

Here's another tip — the digits on the <u>bottom</u> of the fraction should always <u>add up</u> to the number on the <u>top</u>.

Some Binomials contain More Complicated Expressions

The binomials so far have all had a <u>1</u> in the brackets — things get tricky when there's a <u>number other than 1</u>. Don't panic, though. The method is the same as before once you've done a bit of <u>factorising</u>.

Example: What is the coefficient of x^4 in the expansion of $(2 + 5x)^7$?

Factorising $(2 + 5x)$ gives $2(1 + \frac{5}{2}x)$

So, $(2 + 5x)^7$ gives $2^7(1 + \frac{5}{2}x)^7$

It's really easy to forget the first bit (here it's 2^7) — you've been warned...

$$(2 + 5x)^7 = 2^7(1 + \frac{5}{2}x)^7$$

$$= 2^7[1 + 7(\frac{5}{2}x) + \frac{7 \times 6}{1 \times 2}(\frac{5}{2}x)^2 + \frac{7 \times 6 \times 5}{1 \times 2 \times 3}(\frac{5}{2}x)^3 + \frac{7 \times 6 \times 5 \times 4}{1 \times 2 \times 3 \times 4}(\frac{5}{2}x)^4 + ...]$$

Here's the one you want.

The coefficient of x^4 will be $2^7 \times \frac{7!}{4!3!}\left(\frac{5}{2}\right)^4 = 175000$

Don't forget the 2^7.

So, there's <u>no need</u> to work out all of the terms.
In fact, you could have gone <u>directly</u> to the term in x^4 by using the method on page 26.

> Note: The question asked for the <u>coefficient of x^4</u> in the expansion, so <u>don't include any x's</u> in your answer. If you'd been asked for the <u>term in x^4</u> in the expansion, then you <u>should</u> have included the x^4 in your answer.
> <u>Always</u> read the question very carefully.

Pascal was fine at maths but rubbish at music — he only played the triangle...

You can use your calculator to work out these tricky fractions — you use the ^nC_r button (though it could be called something else on your calculator). So to work out $^{20}C_7$, press '20', then press the ^nC_r button, then press '7', and then finish with '='. Now work out $^{15}C_7$ and $^{15}C_8$ — you should get the same answers, since they're both $\frac{15!}{7!8!}$.

Section Four Revision Questions

What's that I hear you cry? You want revision questions — and lots of them. Well it just so happens I've got a few here. Loads of questions on sequences, series and binomial expansions.

With sequences and series, get a clear idea in your head before you start, or you could get to the end of the question and realise the series is arithmetic, not geometric. That would be bad.

1) A sequence has an nth term of $n^2 + 3$. Find a) the first four terms, and b) the 20th term.

2) A sequence is defined by $x_{n+1} = 3x_n - 2$, $x_1 = 4$. Find x_2, x_3 and x_4.

3) The recurrence relation of a sequence is $x_{n+1} = \dfrac{3x_n}{4} + 7$. Find the limit as $n \to \infty$.

4) Find the sum of the series that begins with 5, 8, ... and ends with 65.

5) A series has 1st term 7 and 5th term 23. Find:
   a) the common difference,
   b) the 15th term,
   c) the sum of the first ten terms.

6) A series has seventh term 36 and tenth term 30. Find the sum of the first five terms and the nth term.

7) Find: a) $\displaystyle\sum_{n=1}^{20}(3n-1)$

   b) $\displaystyle\sum_{n=1}^{10}(48-5n)$.

8) For the sequence 2, –6, 18, ..., find the 10th term.

9) For the sequence 24, 12, 6, ..., find:
   a) the common ratio,
   b) the seventh term,
   c) the sum to infinity.

10) A geometric progression and an arithmetic progression both begin with 2, 6, ...
    Which term of the arithmetic progression will be equal to the fifth term of the geometric progression?

11) Find the coefficient of x^2 in the expansion of $(2 + 3x)^5$.

Differentiating x^n

Differentiation is one of those topics that you've just <u>got</u> to get your head round — but luckily it's not too bad really. So relax, take a deep breath, clear your mind of any distracting thoughts, and then engrave this formula upon your heart.

The **Differentiation Formula** works for **Any n**

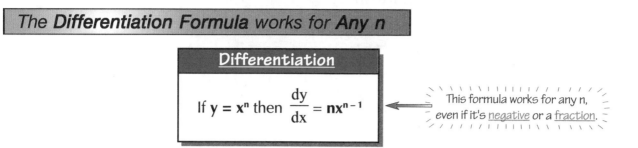

Differentiation

If **y = x^n** then $\dfrac{dy}{dx}$ = **nx^{n-1}**

This formula works for any n, even if it's <u>negative</u> or a <u>fraction</u>.

So if you've got an expression that can be written as a power of x, then differentiating it is easy. And it doesn't matter how fiddly or awkward the power is (it can be negative, a fraction... whatever), the formula still works. So that's good news...

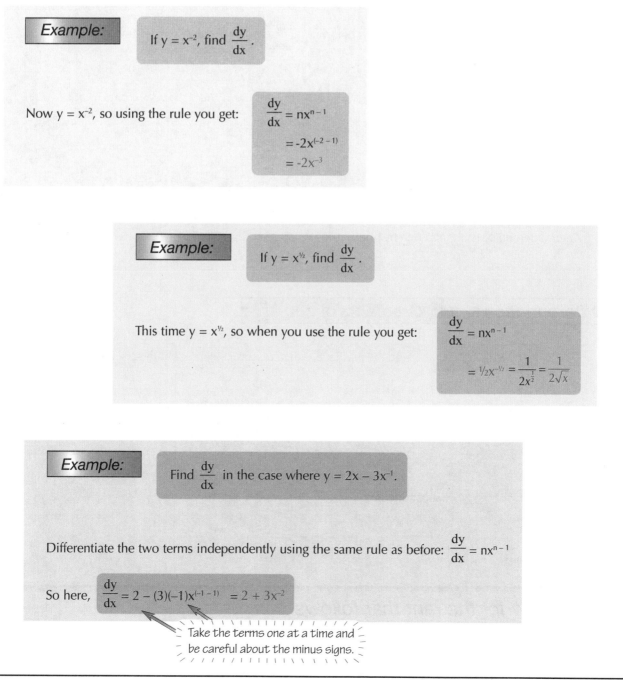

Example:

If $y = x^{-2}$, find $\dfrac{dy}{dx}$.

Now $y = x^{-2}$, so using the rule you get:

$$\frac{dy}{dx} = nx^{n-1}$$
$$= -2x^{(-2-1)}$$
$$= -2x^{-3}$$

Example:

If $y = x^{\frac{1}{2}}$, find $\dfrac{dy}{dx}$.

This time $y = x^{\frac{1}{2}}$, so when you use the rule you get:

$$\frac{dy}{dx} = nx^{n-1}$$
$$= \tfrac{1}{2}x^{-\frac{1}{2}} = \frac{1}{2x^{\frac{1}{2}}} = \frac{1}{2\sqrt{x}}$$

Example:

Find $\dfrac{dy}{dx}$ in the case where $y = 2x - 3x^{-1}$.

Differentiate the two terms independently using the same rule as before: $\dfrac{dy}{dx} = nx^{n-1}$

So here, $\dfrac{dy}{dx} = 2 - (3)(-1)x^{(-1-1)} = 2 + 3x^{-2}$

Take the terms one at a time and be careful about the minus signs.

Differentiating xⁿ

(rendered as) Differentiating x^n

Index Notation makes Fractional Powers easier to work with

To differentiate some functions you'll need to rewrite them in <u>index notation</u> first.

Remember the rules of indices:

Rules of Indices

$$\frac{1}{x^n} = x^{-n} \qquad \sqrt[b]{(x^a)} = x^{\frac{a}{b}}$$

Examples: Differentiate each function with respect to x:

a) $\sqrt[3]{x}$ b) $\dfrac{2}{x^3}$ c) $\dfrac{4}{x^2} - \dfrac{3}{\sqrt{x}}$

a) First rewrite in index notation: $\sqrt[3]{x} = x^{\frac{1}{3}}$

Now differentiate using the same rule as before: $\dfrac{dy}{dx} = \dfrac{1}{3}x^{(\frac{1}{3}-1)} = \dfrac{1}{3}x^{-\frac{2}{3}} = \dfrac{1}{3\sqrt[3]{x^2}}$

b) As before, rewrite using index notation: $\dfrac{2}{x^3} = 2x^{-3}$

Differentiating gives: $\dfrac{dy}{dx} = (2)(-3)x^{(-3-1)} = -6x^{-4} = \dfrac{-6}{x^4}$

> Turn the index notation back into a <u>fraction</u> at the end.

c) Each term must be put into the correct form: $\dfrac{4}{x^2} - \dfrac{3}{\sqrt{x}} = 4x^{-2} - 3x^{-\frac{1}{2}}$

> $\sqrt{x} = x^{\frac{1}{2}}$ so $\dfrac{1}{\sqrt{x}} = x^{-\frac{1}{2}}$

Then differentiate each term one by one: $\dfrac{dy}{dx} = (4)(-2)x^{(-2-1)} - (3)(-\frac{1}{2})x^{(-\frac{1}{2}-1)} = -8x^{-3} + \dfrac{3}{2}x^{-\frac{3}{2}} = -\dfrac{8}{x^3} + \dfrac{3}{2\sqrt{x^3}}$

Use Differentiation to find Gradients of curves

Example: Find the gradient of the curve $y = 4x^{\frac{3}{4}} + x^{-1}$ at the point (1,5).

> $n - 1 = \frac{3}{4} - 1 = -\frac{1}{4}$

To find the gradient, first differentiate: $\dfrac{dy}{dx} = (4 \times \frac{3}{4})x^{-\frac{1}{4}} + (-1)x^{-2}$

$$= 3x^{-\frac{1}{4}} - x^{-2}$$

Now substitute in x = 1: $\dfrac{dy}{dx} = (3)(1^{-\frac{1}{4}}) - (1^{-2})$

> You only need the <u>x-value</u> of the point (1,5).

$$= 3 - 1$$
$$= 2$$

I apologise now for the rant that follows...

Practice is the key. So differentiate any x^n formulas you see — make it your mission in life to differentiate. Differentiate x^n things until you can do it in your sleep. Even if you're not really sure what differentiation actually means, you'll still get marks in the Exam for knowing how to do it. And there's only <u>one</u> formula. So there's absolutely <u>no excuse</u> for not knowing it.

Section Five Revision Questions

Well, that wasn't exactly the longest section in the world, was it. By my reckoning, that section consisted of... hmm, let me see... one formula. And an easy one at that. So don't go putting on that "life's really unfair" face and complaining about how hard you've got it — I'm not listening. Just make sure you know how to use the formula to differentiate powers of x — and by that I mean <u>any</u> power. These questions below should help — you should be able to answer them all using your new magic "differentiate any power of x — even tough ones" formula. If you struggle, then read the last two pages again and find out where you're going wrong, then have another go. You should be able to do them all. No excuses.

1) Differentiate each of the following functions:

   a) $y = x^{-4}$ b) $y = 3x^{1/2}$ c) $f(x) = 4x^2 - 3x^{-3}$

2) For each curve find (i) $\dfrac{dy}{dx}$ and (ii) the gradient at the given point:

   a) $y = 3\sqrt{x} + \dfrac{4}{x}$ at point (4,7) b) $y = \dfrac{2}{x^2} + \dfrac{3}{x^3}$ at point (1,5)

3) a) Verify that the graphs $y = 4 - x$ and $y = \dfrac{2}{\sqrt{x}} + 1$ intersect at (1,3)

   b) Differentiate $y = \dfrac{2}{\sqrt{x}} + 1$

   c) Find the gradient of $y = \dfrac{2}{\sqrt{x}} + 1$ at (1,3)

Integration

Integration... as if you haven't suffered enough already. No, I'm just joking — it's no harder than differentiation.

Up the power by **One** — then **Divide** by it

The formula below tells you how to <u>integrate</u> any power of x (except x⁻¹).

Integration

$$\int x^n dx = \frac{x^{n+1}}{n+1} + C$$

This is an indefinite integral — it doesn't have any limits (numbers) next to the integral sign.

You can't do this to $\frac{1}{x} = x^{-1}$. When you increase the power by 1 (to get <u>zero</u>) and then divide by zero — you get big problems.

In a nutshell, this says:

To integrate a power of x: (i) Increase the power by one
— then divide by it.

and (ii) Stick a constant on the end.

Examples: Use the integration formula...

① For '<u>normal</u>' powers,

$$\int x^3 dx = \frac{x^4}{4} + C$$

Increase the power to 4...

...and then divide by 4.

② For <u>negative</u> powers,

$$\int \frac{1}{x^3} dx = \int x^{-3} dx$$
$$= \frac{x^{-2}}{-2} + C$$
$$= -\frac{1}{2x^2} + C$$

Increase the power by 1 to –2....

...and then divide by –2.

③ For <u>fractional</u> powers,

$$\int \sqrt[3]{x^4} dx = \int x^{\frac{4}{3}} dx$$
$$= \frac{x^{\frac{7}{3}}}{(7/3)} + C$$
$$= \frac{3\sqrt[3]{x^7}}{7} + C$$

Add 1 to the power...

...then divide by this new power.

④ And for complicated looking stuff...

$$\int \left(3x^2 - \frac{2}{\sqrt{x}} + \frac{7}{x^2}\right) dx = \int \left(3x^2 - 2x^{-\frac{1}{2}} + 7x^{-2}\right) dx$$
$$= \frac{3x^3}{3} - \frac{2x^{\frac{1}{2}}}{\frac{1}{2}} + \frac{7x^{-1}}{-1} + C$$
$$= x^3 - 4\sqrt{x} - \frac{7}{x} + C$$

Do each of these bits separately.

⑤ And if the question has limits, put them in just like you've done before.

$$\int_1^4 \left(\sqrt{x} - \frac{1}{3x^2}\right) dx = \int_1^4 \left(x^{\frac{1}{2}} - \frac{1}{3}x^{-2}\right) dx$$

Change the powers to ½ and -2.

$$= \left[\frac{x^{\frac{3}{2}}}{\frac{3}{2}} - \frac{1}{3}\left(\frac{x^{-1}}{-1}\right)\right]_1^4$$

Integrate, put in the limits of 4 and 1, and subtract.

$$= \left[\frac{2}{3}x^{\frac{3}{2}} + \frac{1}{3x}\right]_1^4$$
$$= \left[\left(\frac{2}{3} \times 4^{\frac{3}{2}} + \frac{1}{3 \times 4}\right) - \left(\frac{2}{3} \times 1^{\frac{3}{2}} + \frac{1}{3}\right)\right]$$
$$= \left[\left(\frac{16}{3} + \frac{1}{12}\right) - \left(\frac{2}{3} + \frac{1}{3}\right)\right]$$
$$= \frac{53}{12}$$

<u>Check your answers:</u>
You can check you've integrated properly by <u>differentiating</u> the <u>answer</u> — you should end up with the thing you started with.

Integration

Integration is the opposite of differentiation. If you differentiate something and then integrate the result, you get back to what you started with (give or take a constant).

Find **Curves** and **Areas** by **Integrating**

Add a constant of integration if your integral doesn't have limits (like when you know a curve's derivative, and you want to find the equation of the curve itself).

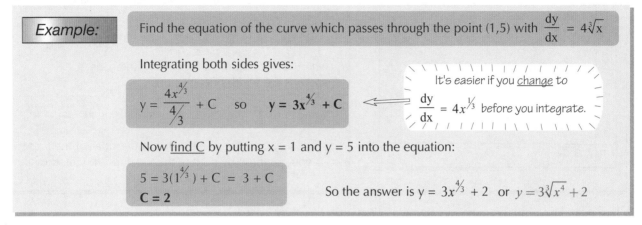

Example: Find the equation of the curve which passes through the point (1,5) with $\frac{dy}{dx} = 4\sqrt[3]{x}$

Integrating both sides gives:

$$y = \frac{4x^{4/3}}{4/3} + C \quad \text{so} \quad y = 3x^{4/3} + C$$

It's easier if you change to $\frac{dy}{dx} = 4x^{1/3}$ before you integrate.

Now find C by putting x = 1 and y = 5 into the equation:

$$5 = 3(1^{4/3}) + C = 3 + C$$
$$C = 2$$

So the answer is $y = 3x^{4/3} + 2$ or $y = 3\sqrt[3]{x^4} + 2$

But if your integral's got limits (like when you're finding the area under a graph), don't bother with the constant.

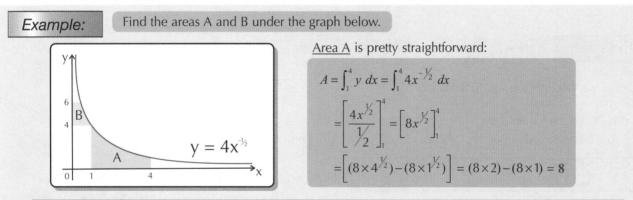

Example: Find the areas A and B under the graph below.

Area A is pretty straightforward:

$$A = \int_1^4 y\,dx = \int_1^4 4x^{-1/2}\,dx$$
$$= \left[\frac{4x^{1/2}}{1/2}\right]_1^4 = \left[8x^{1/2}\right]_1^4$$
$$= \left[(8 \times 4^{1/2}) - (8 \times 1^{1/2})\right] = (8 \times 2) - (8 \times 1) = 8$$

Graph shows $y = 4x^{-1/2}$ with area A between x = 1 and x = 4, and area B between y = 4 and y = 6.

Area B is a bit nastier...

The integrals you've found so far have been of the form $\int_a^b y\,dx$ (the 'dx' means you're integrating with respect to x), which gives you the area between a curve and the x-axis between x = a and x = b. So you write y in terms of x and integrate...
This time, you need the area between a curve and the y-axis, so you integrate with respect to y (i.e. use an integral of the form $\int_c^d x\,dy$, where the limits show the maximum and minimum values of y — here y = 4 and y = 6).
With 'dy' integrals, you have to write everything in terms of y before you can integrate...

So here $B = \int_4^6 x\,dy$. First you need to put x in terms of y: $y = 4x^{-1/2} = \frac{4}{\sqrt{x}}$, so $y^2 = \frac{16}{x}$, i.e. $x = \frac{16}{y^2} = 16y^{-2}$

Right then, away we go... $B = \int_4^6 16y^{-2}dy$

$$= \left[\frac{16y^{-1}}{-1}\right]_4^6 = \left[\frac{-16}{y}\right]_4^6$$
$$= \left[\left(\frac{-16}{6}\right) - \left(\frac{-16}{4}\right)\right] = -\frac{8}{3} + 4 = \frac{4}{3}$$

With 'dy' integrals, increase the power and divide by it in the normal way — except this time they're powers of y rather than x.

Bob's your uncle.

What we hope ever to do with ease, we must learn first to do with diligence...

That's what Dr Johnson reckoned, anyway. And he knew a thing or two, I can tell you. I don't know exactly what he had in mind when he said it, admittedly, but it's true about integration anyway. At first, you'll need all your powers of concentration to avoid making mistakes. But with a bit of practice, it'll become as easy as falling off a log.

34

The Trapezium Rule

Sometimes <u>integrals</u> can be just <u>too hard</u> to do using the normal methods — then you need to know other ways to solve them. That's where the <u>Trapezium Rule</u> comes in.

The *Trapezium Rule* is Used to Find the *Approximate Area* Under a Curve

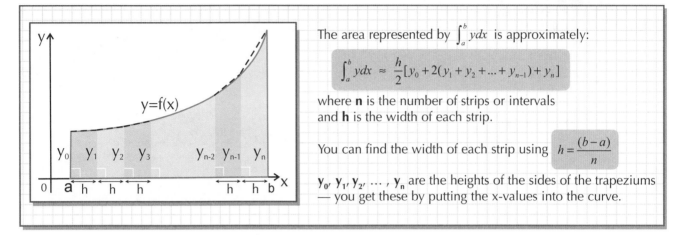

The area represented by $\int_a^b y\,dx$ is approximately:

$$\int_a^b y\,dx \approx \frac{h}{2}[y_0 + 2(y_1 + y_2 + ... + y_{n-1}) + y_n]$$

where **n** is the number of strips or intervals and **h** is the width of each strip.

You can find the width of each strip using $h = \frac{(b-a)}{n}$

$y_0, y_1, y_2, ... , y_n$ are the heights of the sides of the trapeziums — you get these by putting the x-values into the curve.

So basically the formula for approximating $\int_a^b y\,dx$ works like this:

'Add the first and last heights $(y_0 + y_n)$ and add this to <u>twice</u> all the other heights added up — then multiply by $\frac{h}{2}$.'

| Example: | Find an approximate value for $\int_0^2 \sqrt{4-x^2}\,dx$ using 4 strips. Give your answer to 4 s.f. |

Start by working out the width of each strip: $h = \frac{(b-a)}{n} = \frac{(2-0)}{4} = 0.5$

This means the x-values are $x_0 = 0$, $x_1 = 0.5$, $x_2 = 1$, $x_3 = 1.5$ and $x_4 = 2$ (the question specifies 4 strips, so n = 4). Set up a table and work out the y-values or heights using the equation in the integral.

x	$y = \sqrt{4-x^2}$
$x_0 = 0$	$y_0 = \sqrt{4-0^2} = 2$
$x_1 = 0.5$	$y_1 = \sqrt{4-0.5^2} = \sqrt{3.75} = 1.936491673$
$x_2 = 1.0$	$y_2 = \sqrt{4-1.0^2} = \sqrt{3} = 1.732050808$
$x_3 = 1.5$	$y_3 = \sqrt{4-1.5^2} = \sqrt{1.75} = 1.322875656$
$x_4 = 2.0$	$y_4 = \sqrt{4-2.0^2} = 0$

Now put all the y-values into the formula with h and n:

$$\int_a^b y\,dx \approx \frac{0.5}{2}[2 + 2(1.936491673 + 1.732050808 + 1.322875656) + 0]$$
$$\approx 0.25[2 + 2 \times 4.991418137]$$
$$\approx 2.996 \text{ to 4 s.f.}$$

Watch out — if they ask you to work out a question with 5 y-values (or '<u>ordinates</u>') then this is the <u>same</u> as 4 strips. The x-values usually go up in <u>nice jumps</u> — if they don't then <u>check</u> your calculations carefully.

The *Approximation* might be an *Overestimate* or an *Underestimate*

It all depends on the shape of the curve...

The estimate is <u>less</u> than the real areas.

The estimate is <u>more</u> than the real areas.

The Trapezium Rule

These are usually popular questions with examiners — as long as you're careful there are <u>plenty of marks</u> to be had.

The Trapezium Rule is in the Formula Booklet

...so don't try any heroics — always <u>look it up</u> and use it with these questions.

Example: Use the trapezium rule with 7 ordinates to find an approximation to $\int_1^{2.2} 2\log_{10} x \, dx$

Remember, <u>7 ordinates</u> means <u>6 strips</u> — so n = 6.

Calculate the width of the strips: $h = \dfrac{(b-a)}{n} = \dfrac{(2.2-1)}{6} = 0.2$

Set up a table and work out the y-values using $y = 2\log_{10} x$:

x	$y = 2\log_{10} x$
$x_0 = 1.0$	$y_0 = 2\log_{10} 1 = 0$
$x_1 = 1.2$	$y_1 = 2\log_{10} 1.2 = 0.15836$
$x_2 = 1.4$	$y_2 = 0.29226$
$x_3 = 1.6$	$y_3 = 0.40824$
$x_4 = 1.8$	$y_4 = 0.51055$
$x_5 = 2.0$	$y_5 = 0.60206$
$x_6 = 2.2$	$y_6 = 0.68485$

Putting all these values in the formula gives: $y_6 = 2\log_{10} b = 0.68485$

$$\int_a^b y\,dx \approx \frac{0.2}{2}[0 + 2(0.15836 + 0.29226 + 0.40824 + 0.51055 + 0.60206) + 0.68485]$$

$$\approx 0.1 \times [0.68485 + 2 \times 1.97147]$$

$$\approx 0.462777$$

$$\approx 0.463 \text{ to 3 d.p.}$$

Example: Use the trapezium rule with 8 intervals to find an approximation to $\int_0^\pi \sin x \, dx$

Whenever you get a calculus question using <u>trig functions</u>, you <u>have</u> to use <u>radians</u>. You'll probably be given a limit with π in, which is a pretty good reminder.

There are 8 intervals, so n = 8.

Keep your x-values in terms of π.

Calculate the width of the strips: $h = \dfrac{(b-a)}{n} = \dfrac{(\pi-0)}{8} = \dfrac{\pi}{8}$

Set up a table and work out the y-values:

x	$y = \sin x$
$x_0 = 0$	$y_0 = \sin 0 = 0$
$x_1 = \dfrac{\pi}{8}$	$y_1 = 0.38268$
$x_2 = \dfrac{\pi}{4}$	$y_2 = 0.70711$
$x_3 = \dfrac{3\pi}{8}$	$y_3 = 0.92388$
$x_4 = \dfrac{\pi}{2}$	$y_4 = 1$
$x_5 = \dfrac{5\pi}{8}$	$y_5 = 0.92388$
$x_6 = \dfrac{3\pi}{4}$	$y_6 = 0.70711$
$x_7 = \dfrac{7\pi}{8}$	$y_7 = 0.38268$
$x_8 = \pi$	$y_8 = 0$

So, putting all this in the formula gives:

$$\int_a^b y\,dx \approx \frac{1}{2}\cdot\frac{\pi}{8}[0 + 2(0.38268 + 0.70711 + 0.92388 + 1 + 0.92388 + 0.70711 + 0.38268) + 0]$$

$$\approx \frac{\pi}{16}[2 \times 5.02734]$$

$$\approx 1.9742$$

$$\approx 1.974 \text{ to 3 d.p.}$$

Maths rhyming slang #3: Dribble and drool — Trapezium rule...

Take your time with Trapezium Rule questions — it's so easy to make a mistake with all those numbers flying around. Make a nice table showing all your ordinates (careful — this is always one more than the number of strips). Then add up y_1 to y_{n-1} and multiply the answer by 2. Add on y_0 and y_n. Finally, multiply what you've got so far by the width of a strip and <u>divide by 2</u>. It's a good idea to write down what you get after each stage, by the way — then if you press the wrong button (easily done) you'll be able to pick up from where you went wrong. They're not hard — just fiddly.

Section Six Revision Questions

They think it's all over...

1) Integrate the following:

   a) $\int 10x^4 dx$ b) $\int \frac{4}{x^3} dx$ c) $\int (3x^3 + 2x^2) dx$ d) $\int 4\sqrt[3]{x}\, dx$ e) $\int \left(6x^5 - \frac{2}{x^2} + \sqrt{x} \right) dx$

2) Find the equation of the curve which passes through (1,0) with $\frac{dy}{dx} = \sqrt{x} + \frac{2}{x^2}$

3) Evaluate the following:

   a) $\int_1^2 \left(\frac{8}{x^5} + \frac{3}{\sqrt{x}} \right) dx$ b) $\int_1^6 \frac{3}{y^2} dy$

4) Find area A from the graph below:

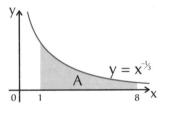

5) Use the trapezium rule with n intervals to estimate:

   a) $\int_0^3 (9 - x^2)^{\frac{1}{2}} dx$ with $n = 3$

   b) $\int_{0.2}^{1.2} x^{x^2} dx;\ n = 5$

...it is now.

Core 2 Mathematics — Practice Exam One

Give non-exact numerical answers correct to 3 significant figures, unless a
different degree of accuracy is specified in the question or is clearly appropriate.

1 (i) By sketching the graph of $y = \tan 2t$ for a suitable range of t, determine the number of solutions to the equation
$\tan 2t = k$ in the range $0° \le t < 360°$, where k is any number. [3]
(ii) Solve the equation $\sin 2t = \sqrt{2} \cos 2t$, giving all the solutions in the range $0° \le t < 360°$. [4]

2 (i) Write down the value of $\log_3 3$ [1]
(ii) Given that $\log_a \chi = \log_a 4 + 3 \log_a 2$ show that $\chi = 32$ [3]

3 (i) Write down the exact value of $36^{-\frac{1}{2}}$ [2]

(ii) Simplify $\dfrac{a^6 \times a^3}{\sqrt{a^4}} \div a^{\frac{1}{2}}$ [2]

(iii) Express $\left(5\sqrt{5} + 2\sqrt{3}\right)^2$ in the form $a + b\sqrt{c}$, where a, b and c are integers to be found. [2]

(iv) Rationalise the denominator of $\dfrac{10}{\sqrt{5}+1}$. [3]

4 (i) Sketch the curve $y = \dfrac{1}{x^2}$ for $x > 0$. [1]

(ii) Show that $\displaystyle\int_1^\infty \dfrac{1}{x^2}\,dx = 1$. [2]

(iii) Find the equation of f(x), where f(x) is the tangent to the graph of $y = \dfrac{1}{x^2}$ at the point where $x = 1$. [2]

(iv) Find k < 1 such that $\displaystyle\int_0^k f(x)\,dx = 1$. Give your answer using surds. [3]

5 The derivative of a function is given by $\dfrac{dy}{dx} = \dfrac{1}{2}x^2 - \dfrac{3}{\sqrt{x}}$

(i) Find an expression for y if the graph of y against x is to pass through the point $\left(1, \dfrac{1}{6}\right)$. [4]

(ii) Evaluate $\displaystyle\int_0^1 y\,dx$. [5]

6 (i) An ascending arithmetic series has first term a and common difference d.
(a) Write down expressions for u_n, u_{n+1} and u_{n+2}, the nth, $(n+1)^{th}$ and $(n+2)^{th}$ terms in the series respectively. [2]
(b) By making the substitution $x = a + nd$, write these expressions in terms of x and d only. [4]
(c) If the sum of u_n, u_{n+1} and u_{n+2} is 36, and their product is 960, find the values of x and d. [4]
(d) If u_n, u_{n+1} and u_{n+2} above are the first three terms of the series, find the value of u_1, and hence
write down an expression for u_n in terms of n. [3]
(ii) Find S_{10}, the sum of the first ten terms of the series. [3]
(iii) By considering the formula for S_n and the formula for the sum $\sigma_n = 1 + 2 + 3 + ... + n$, find an expression
for the difference $S_n - \sigma_n$, giving your answer in as simple a form as possible. [4]

7 (i) (a) Show that $\log_3 9 = 2$ [1]

(b) Find the value of $\log_3 (9^3)$ [2]

(c) Find the value of $\log_3 \dfrac{1}{\sqrt[3]{9}}$ [3]

(ii) Solve:

(a) $\log_2 x = 7$ [1]
(b) $10^{4x} = 300$ [2]
(c) $6^x = 40$ [3]

8 The diagram opposite shows a sector of a circle of radius r cm and angle 120°.
The length of the arc of the sector is 40 cm.
(i) Write 120° in radians. [1]
(ii) Show that $r \approx 19.1$ cm. [2]
(iii) Find the area of the sector to the nearest square centimetre. [3]

40 cm

120°

r

Paper 1 Q1 — Trigonometry

1 (i) By sketching the graph of $y = \tan 2t$ for a suitable range of t, determine the number of solutions to the equation

$\tan 2t = k$ in the range $0° \le t < 360°$, where k is any number.   [3]

(ii) Solve the equation $\sin 2t = \sqrt{2} \cos 2t$, giving all the solutions in the range $0° \le t < 360°$.   [4]

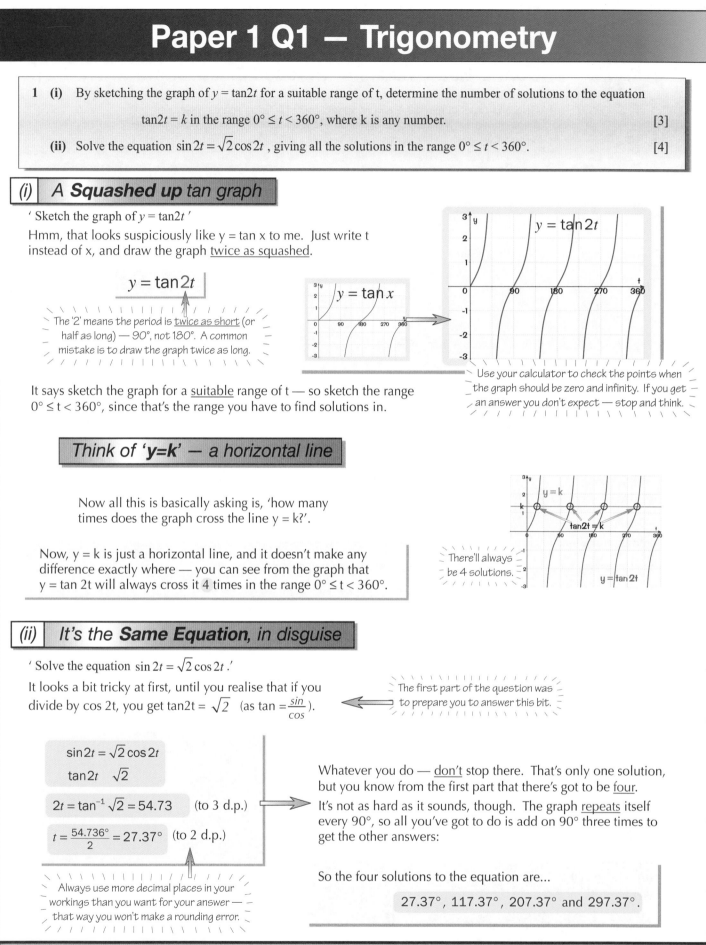

(i) A **Squashed up** tan graph

' Sketch the graph of $y = \tan 2t$ '

Hmm, that looks suspiciously like $y = \tan x$ to me. Just write t instead of x, and draw the graph <u>twice as squashed</u>.

$$y = \tan 2t$$

The '2' means the period is <u>twice as short</u> (or half as long) — 90°, not 180°. A common mistake is to draw the graph twice as long.

It says sketch the graph for a <u>suitable</u> range of t — so sketch the range $0° \le t < 360°$, since that's the range you have to find solutions in.

Use your calculator to check the points when the graph should be zero and infinity. If you get an answer you don't expect — stop and think.

Think of '**y=k**' — a horizontal line

Now all this is basically asking is, 'how many times does the graph cross the line y = k?'.

Now, y = k is just a horizontal line, and it doesn't make any difference exactly where — you can see from the graph that y = tan 2t will always cross it **4** times in the range $0° \le t < 360°$.

There'll always be 4 solutions.

(ii) It's the **Same Equation**, in disguise

' Solve the equation $\sin 2t = \sqrt{2} \cos 2t$.'

It looks a bit tricky at first, until you realise that if you divide by cos 2t, you get $\tan 2t = \sqrt{2}$ (as $\tan = \frac{\sin}{\cos}$).

The first part of the question was to prepare you to answer this bit.

$$\sin 2t = \sqrt{2} \cos 2t$$
$$\tan 2t \quad \sqrt{2}$$

$2t = \tan^{-1}\sqrt{2} = 54.73$ (to 3 d.p.)

$t = \frac{54.736°}{2} = 27.37°$ (to 2 d.p.)

Always use more decimal places in your workings than you want for your answer — that way you won't make a rounding error.

Whatever you do — <u>don't</u> stop there. That's only one solution, but you know from the first part that there's got to be <u>four</u>.

It's not as hard as it sounds, though. The graph <u>repeats</u> itself every 90°, so all you've got to do is add on 90° three times to get the other answers:

So the four solutions to the equation are...

$$27.37°, \ 117.37°, \ 207.37° \text{ and } 297.37°.$$

Trig or happy? Trig or treat? Trig or finger? It's just trig-tastic...

There are two important things to be learnt here: Firstly, make sure you know all those standard graphs — then the first part of the question really should be easy. And secondly, if you're stuck on the last part of the question, always look at the earlier bits for hints — it's a pretty safe bet there's going to be some kind of connection that'll help.

Paper 1 Q2 — Logs

> **2 (i)** Write down the value of $\log_3 3$ [1]
>
> **(ii)** Given that $\log_a \chi = \log_a 4 + 3\log_a 2$ show that $\chi = 32$ [3]

(i) $Log_3 3$ — Some Marks are a Giveaway...

'Write down the value of $\log_3 3$'

This isn't a trick question — they're just checking you know what log means. From page 15 you should (hopefully) remember that:

> $\log_a b = c$ means the same as $a^c = b$
>
> That means that $\boxed{\log_a a = 1}$ and $\log_a 1 = 0$

From that bit, it's pretty easy to work out that $\log_3 3 = 1$.

(In other words, $3^1 = 3$, which you should also know from the laws of indices that you did in Core 1.)

(ii) For Log Equations you need to Learn the Log Laws

You'll get the first mark for showing you can use one of the <u>laws of logarithms</u> and the other for successfully getting $\chi = 32$.

OK, let's get stuck in...

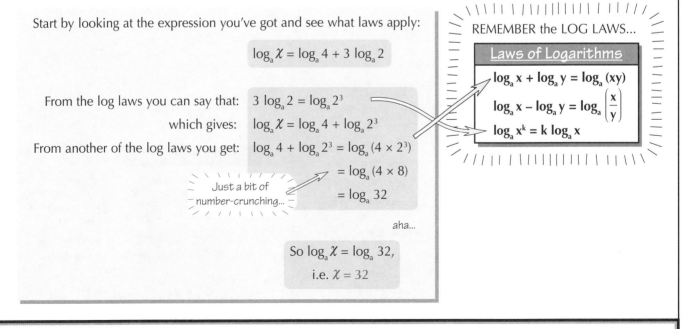

Start by looking at the expression you've got and see what laws apply:

$$\log_a \chi = \log_a 4 + 3\log_a 2$$

REMEMBER the LOG LAWS...

Laws of Logarithms

$$\log_a x + \log_a y = \log_a (xy)$$
$$\log_a x - \log_a y = \log_a \left(\frac{x}{y}\right)$$
$$\log_a x^k = k\log_a x$$

From the log laws you can say that: $3\log_a 2 = \log_a 2^3$

which gives: $\log_a \chi = \log_a 4 + \log_a 2^3$

From another of the log laws you get: $\log_a 4 + \log_a 2^3 = \log_a (4 \times 2^3)$

$$= \log_a (4 \times 8)$$

Just a bit of number-crunching...

$$= \log_a 32$$

aha...

So $\log_a \chi = \log_a 32$,

i.e. $\chi = 32$

AS Maths — (nearly) as easy as falling off a log...

OK, logs aren't the easiest thing in the world, but this is a straightforward question so quit complaining. The best way to prepare for an exam question on logs is to *LEARN THE LOG LAWS*. Whether or not you can apply those laws is kind of irrelevant if you don't know them in the first place. So I repeat: *LEARN THE LOG LAWS*... and *then* practise using them.

Paper 1 Q3 — Powers and Surds

3   (i)   Write down the exact value of $36^{-\frac{1}{2}}$ [2]

    (ii)   Simplify $\dfrac{a^6 \times a^3}{\sqrt{a^4}} \div a^{\frac{1}{2}}$ [2]

    (iii)   Express $\left(5\sqrt{5} + 2\sqrt{3}\right)^2$ in the form $a + b\sqrt{c}$, where a, b and c are integers to be found.   [2]

    (iv)   Rationalise the denominator of $\dfrac{10}{\sqrt{5}+1}$.   [3]

(i)   Power Law questions can usually be answered by Rearranging

'Write down the exact value of $36^{-\frac{1}{2}}$.'

With Power Law questions, you usually just have to remember a couple of basic formulas, then do a couple of sums pretty darn carefully. If you've forgotten any of the Laws, they're all on page 4. So, on with the question...

First get rid of the minus in the exponent / power...

$$x^{-n} = \frac{1}{x^n} \longrightarrow 36^{-\frac{1}{2}} = \frac{1}{36^{\frac{1}{2}}}$$

Then deal with the $\frac{1}{2}$.

$$\frac{1}{36^{\frac{1}{2}}} = \frac{1}{\sqrt{36}} \longleftarrow x^{\frac{1}{n}} = \sqrt[n]{x}$$

And finally...

Do a simple square root. $\longrightarrow \dfrac{1}{\sqrt{36}} = \dfrac{1}{6}$

Check Your Answer:

You can check your answer using your calculator. Just enter:

$36 \quad x^y \quad - \quad 0.5 \quad =$

You should get something like this... $\longrightarrow 0.1666667$

...and that's roughly a sixth. $\longrightarrow \dfrac{1}{6}$

(ii)   Simplifying just means Rearranging as well

'Simplify $\dfrac{a^6 \times a^3}{\sqrt{a^4}} \div a^{\frac{1}{2}}$'

When you're simplifying powers, it's a good idea to get them all looking the same. In this example, get the individual bits in the form a^n.

See page 1 for more info on the Power Laws.

First simplify the tricky bit on the bottom of the fraction...

$$\sqrt[m]{a^n} = a^{\frac{n}{m}} \longrightarrow \frac{a^6 \times a^3}{\sqrt{a^4}} \div a^{\frac{1}{2}} = \frac{a^6 \times a^3}{a^2} \div a^{\frac{1}{2}}$$

Then rewrite this so that you're only multiplying things.

$$a^6 \times a^3 \times a^{-2} \times a^{-\frac{1}{2}} \longleftarrow \frac{1}{a^n} = a^{-n}$$

Dividing by a^n is the same as multiplying by a^{-n}.

And then just add all the powers together, to get

$$a^6 \times a^3 \times a^{-2} \times a^{-\frac{1}{2}} = a^{6+3-2-\frac{1}{2}}$$

$$= a^{\frac{13}{2}} \qquad \text{Hurray...}$$

Check Your Answer:

$$\frac{a^6 \times a^3}{\sqrt{a^4}} \div a^{\frac{1}{2}} = a^{6\frac{1}{2}}$$

Check your answer by substituting a value for a.

$$\frac{2^6 \times 2^3}{\sqrt{2^4}} \div 2^{\frac{1}{2}} = 2^{6\frac{1}{2}}$$

Work each power of two out separately.

$$\frac{64 \times 8}{4} \div 1.41421 = 90.509$$

Keep lots of decimal places.

$$90.509 = 90.509$$

If both sides are equal, you've got the right answer.

This may sound stupid, but questions on Power Laws aren't too bad, as long as you obey the Power Laws. It really is that simple.

Paper 1 Q3 — Powers and Surds

(iii) | *Multiply out the brackets — then use the rules for Surds*

'Express $\left(5\sqrt{5} + 2\sqrt{3}\right)^2$ in the form $a + b\sqrt{c}$, where a, b and c are integers to be found.'

Yet again, you've got to simplify and rearrange the equation.

First of all (after the initial shock of "Arrrgghh — surds") you should get rid of the <u>squared sign</u> around the brackets.

Multiply out the brackets first:

<u>Multiply this out like a normal quadratic.</u>

$$\left(5\sqrt{5} + 2\sqrt{3}\right)^2 = \left(5\sqrt{5} + 2\sqrt{3}\right) \times \left(5\sqrt{5} + 2\sqrt{3}\right)$$

$$= \left(5\sqrt{5}\right)^2 + 2\left(5\sqrt{5} \times 2\sqrt{3}\right) + \left(2\sqrt{3}\right)^2$$

This next bit's a tad confusing, I reckon. You've got three terms to deal with, and they're all a little bit nasty.

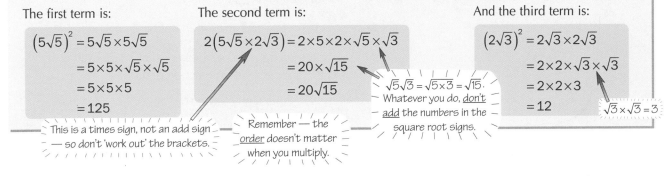

The first term is:

$$\left(5\sqrt{5}\right)^2 = 5\sqrt{5} \times 5\sqrt{5}$$
$$= 5 \times 5 \times \sqrt{5} \times \sqrt{5}$$
$$= 5 \times 5 \times 5$$
$$= 125$$

This is a times sign, not an add sign — so don't 'work out' the brackets.

The second term is:

$$2\left(5\sqrt{5} \times 2\sqrt{3}\right) = 2 \times 5 \times 2 \times \sqrt{5} \times \sqrt{3}$$
$$= 20 \times \sqrt{15}$$
$$= 20\sqrt{15}$$

Remember — the <u>order</u> doesn't matter when you multiply.

$\sqrt{5}\sqrt{3} = \sqrt{5 \times 3} = \sqrt{15}$. Whatever you do, <u>don't</u> add the numbers in the square root signs.

And the third term is:

$$\left(2\sqrt{3}\right)^2 = 2\sqrt{3} \times 2\sqrt{3}$$
$$= 2 \times 2 \times \sqrt{3} \times \sqrt{3}$$
$$= 2 \times 2 \times 3$$
$$= 12$$

$\sqrt{3} \times \sqrt{3} = 3$

Now you've done that, though, you're almost home and dry. All that's left to do is add the three terms together.

So the whole thing's equal to...

$$125 + 20\sqrt{15} + 12 = 137 + 20\sqrt{15}$$

And since 137, 20 and 15 are all <u>integers</u>, this is the final answer to the question.

(iv) | *Rationalise by multiplying top and bottom lines by the Same Thing*

'Rationalise the denominator of $\frac{10}{1 + \sqrt{5}}$.'

Rationalising a denominator means getting rid of surds on the bottom line of a fraction. Sounds hard — but it's easy. The key is to use the <u>difference of two squares</u>. If you've got "$a + \sqrt{b}$" on the bottom line, you have to multiply <u>top</u> and <u>bottom</u> lines by "$a - \sqrt{b}$". This will <u>always</u> get rid of the surd on the bottom (though you may end up with one on the top).

Just change the sign before the surd — and multiply top and bottom lines by it.

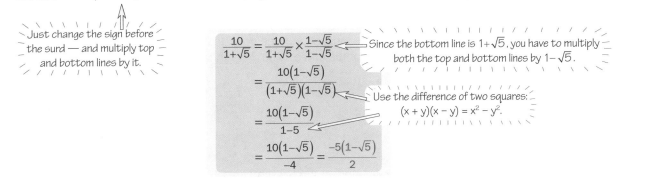

$$\frac{10}{1 + \sqrt{5}} = \frac{10}{1 + \sqrt{5}} \times \frac{1 - \sqrt{5}}{1 - \sqrt{5}}$$

Since the bottom line is $1 + \sqrt{5}$, you have to multiply both the top and bottom lines by $1 - \sqrt{5}$.

$$= \frac{10\left(1 - \sqrt{5}\right)}{\left(1 + \sqrt{5}\right)\left(1 - \sqrt{5}\right)}$$

Use the difference of two squares:
$$(x + y)(x - y) = x^2 - y^2.$$

$$= \frac{10\left(1 - \sqrt{5}\right)}{1 - 5}$$

$$= \frac{10\left(1 - \sqrt{5}\right)}{-4} = \frac{-5\left(1 - \sqrt{5}\right)}{2}$$

Keep your Magic Power Laws close to you at all times...

I don't want to go on and on and start ranting but... hang on a bit, I <u>do</u> want to go on and on, and I <u>do</u> want to rant. The thing is that questions on the Power Laws <u>always</u> come up in the exams and are <u>always</u> worth a <u>good few marks</u>. And those few marks could make the difference between one grade and the next. Think about it — half an hour spent learning these 2 pages really well could move you up a grade. You know it makes sense...

Paper 1 Q4 — Integration and Tangents

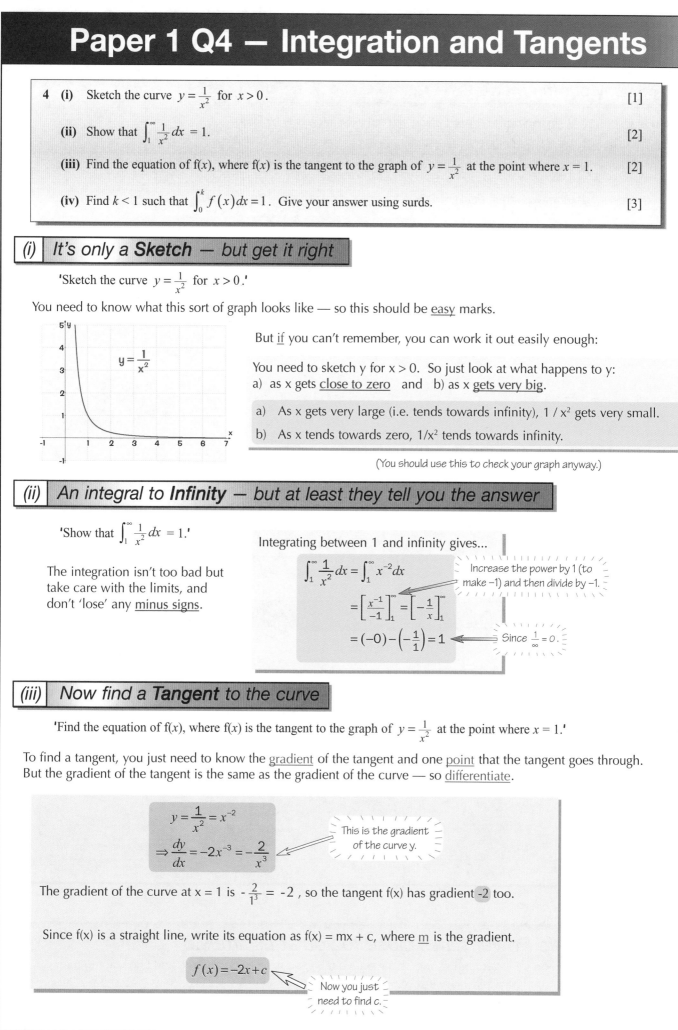

4 (i) Sketch the curve $y = \frac{1}{x^2}$ for $x > 0$. [1]

(ii) Show that $\int_1^{\infty} \frac{1}{x^2} dx = 1$. [2]

(iii) Find the equation of f(x), where f(x) is the tangent to the graph of $y = \frac{1}{x^2}$ at the point where $x = 1$. [2]

(iv) Find $k < 1$ such that $\int_0^k f(x) dx = 1$. Give your answer using surds. [3]

(i) It's only a **Sketch** — but get it right

'Sketch the curve $y = \frac{1}{x^2}$ for $x > 0$.'

You need to know what this sort of graph looks like — so this should be <u>easy</u> marks.

But <u>if</u> you can't remember, you can work it out easily enough:

You need to sketch y for x > 0. So just look at what happens to y:
a) as x gets <u>close to zero</u> and b) as x <u>gets very big</u>.

a) As x gets very large (i.e. tends towards infinity), 1 / x² gets very small.

b) As x tends towards zero, 1/x² tends towards infinity.

(You should use this to check your graph anyway.)

(ii) An integral to **Infinity** — but at least they tell you the answer

'Show that $\int_1^{\infty} \frac{1}{x^2} dx = 1$.'

The integration isn't too bad but take care with the limits, and don't 'lose' any <u>minus signs</u>.

Integrating between 1 and infinity gives...

$$\int_1^{\infty} \frac{1}{x^2} dx = \int_1^{\infty} x^{-2} dx$$

Increase the power by 1 (to make −1) and then divide by −1.

$$= \left[\frac{x^{-1}}{-1} \right]_1^{\infty} = \left[-\frac{1}{x} \right]_1^{\infty}$$

$$= (-0) - \left(-\frac{1}{1} \right) = 1$$

Since $\frac{1}{\infty} = 0$.

(iii) Now find a **Tangent** to the curve

'Find the equation of f(x), where f(x) is the tangent to the graph of $y = \frac{1}{x^2}$ at the point where $x = 1$.'

To find a tangent, you just need to know the <u>gradient</u> of the tangent and one <u>point</u> that the tangent goes through. But the gradient of the tangent is the same as the gradient of the curve — so <u>differentiate</u>.

$$y = \frac{1}{x^2} = x^{-2}$$

$$\Rightarrow \frac{dy}{dx} = -2x^{-3} = -\frac{2}{x^3}$$

This is the gradient of the curve y.

The gradient of the curve at x = 1 is $-\frac{2}{1^3} = -2$, so the tangent f(x) has gradient -2 too.

Since f(x) is a straight line, write its equation as f(x) = mx + c, where <u>m</u> is the gradient.

$$f(x) = -2x + c$$

Now you just need to find c.

Paper 1 Q4 — Integration and Tangents

To find c, you need to use the fact that the tangent <u>touches</u> the curve at the point (1, 1).

The lines meet at the point (1, 1), and so

$$f(x) = -2x + c$$
$$\Rightarrow 1 = (-2 \times 1) + c = -2 + c$$

Since $f(1) = 1$.

$$\Rightarrow c = 3$$

And this means the equation of f(x) is...

$$f(x) = -2x + 3$$
$$\text{i.e.} \quad f(x) = 3 - 2x$$

This means the same but looks a bit neater.

(iv) Another **Integration** — but this time you have to find the **Upper Limit**

'Find $k < 1$ such that $\int_0^k f(x)\,dx = 1$. Give your answer using surds.'

Now you need to find a value less than 1 for k. Just do the integration <u>normally</u> but write k instead of a number...

$$\int_0^k f(x)\,dx = \int_0^k (3 - 2x)\,dx$$
$$= \left[3x - x^2\right]_0^k$$
$$= (3k - k^2) - 0$$
$$= 3k - k^2$$

Don't do anything differently just because you have k instead of a number.

This integral has to be equal to 1, so you need to solve

$$3k - k^2 = 1$$
$$\Rightarrow k^2 - 3k + 1 = 0$$

Since the question asks you to find k such that $\int_0^k f(x)\,dx = 1$.

This is a <u>quadratic</u>, and the question mentions <u>surds</u> — so it doesn't look as though it's going to factorise.

Using the quadratic formula...

$$k = \frac{3 \pm \sqrt{(-3)^2 - 4 \times 1 \times 1}}{2 \times 1}$$
$$= \frac{3 \pm \sqrt{5}}{2}$$

There are two possible values for k here — you have to decide which one you need.

The question says k has to be less than 1 — so use a calculator to work out which of these possible values you need.

So this is the one you need.

$$\frac{3 + \sqrt{5}}{2} = 2.618 \qquad \frac{3 - \sqrt{5}}{2} = 0.382$$

The question asks you to give your final answer in <u>surds</u>, though.

And so the required value of k is

$$k = \frac{3 - \sqrt{5}}{2}$$

f(x)? Can't they think of a better name? Like Trevor. Yes — Trevor The Tangent

Phew. I mean, really... phew. What a stinker. Let's break it down. <u>Part i)</u> — you really should know what graphs like y = kxⁿ look like — but you can work it out anyway if you just choose a few values for x, work out the value of y there, and then plot the points. <u>Part ii)</u> It's just a limit integration. Don't be put off by the ∞ — it only comes into play when you're substituting in the limits at the end (where you have to use the fact that 1/∞ is 0). <u>Part iii)</u> is okay really. Nuff said. <u>Part iv)</u> — well it's long. And you get two answers at the end when you might only expect one. When this happens, have another look at the question and see if you can get rid of one somehow. Here, they only want a value of k that's less than 1 — so you can get rid of the one that's bigger than 1. Obvious, eh? — but easily forgotten in the exam.

Paper 1 Q5 — Calculus

5   The derivative of a function is given by

$$\frac{dy}{dx} = \frac{1}{2}x^2 - \frac{3}{\sqrt{x}}$$

(i)   Find an expression for y if the graph of y against x is to pass through the point $\left(1, \frac{1}{6}\right)$.   [4]

(ii)   Evaluate $\int_0^1 y\,dx$.   [5]

(i)   You just **Integrate** it...

'Find an expression for y if the graph of y against x is to pass through the point $\left(1, \frac{1}{6}\right)$.'

To get an expression for y from an expression for $\frac{dy}{dx}$, you just <u>integrate</u>.

(Integration is the opposite of differentiation, remember.)

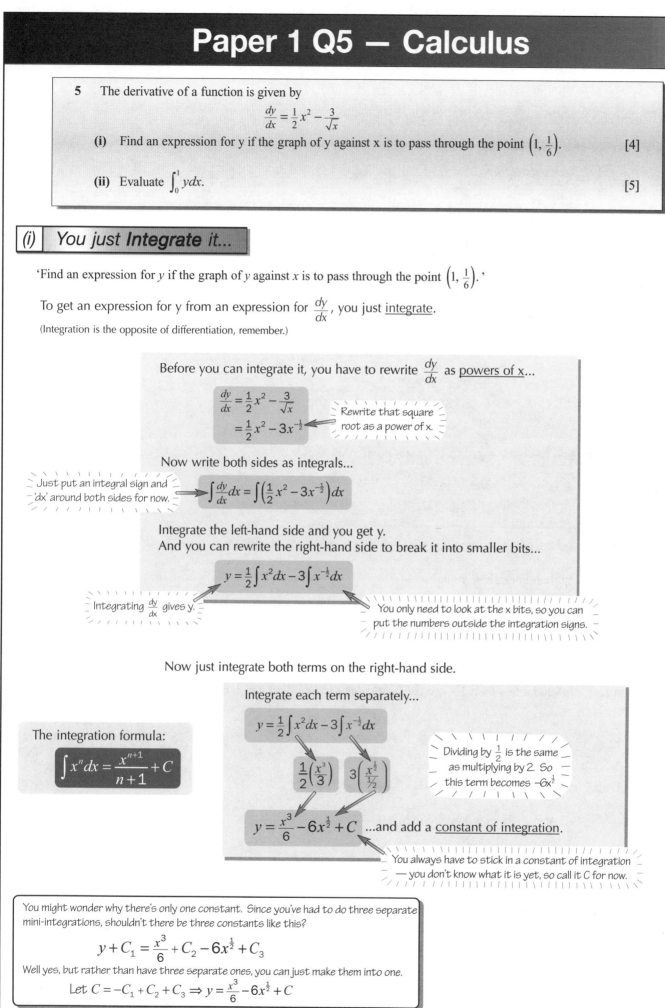

Before you can integrate it, you have to rewrite $\frac{dy}{dx}$ as <u>powers of x</u>...

$$\frac{dy}{dx} = \frac{1}{2}x^2 - \frac{3}{\sqrt{x}}$$
$$= \frac{1}{2}x^2 - 3x^{-\frac{1}{2}}$$

Rewrite that square root as a power of x.

Now write both sides as integrals...

Just put an integral sign and 'dx' around both sides for now.

$$\int \frac{dy}{dx}\,dx = \int\left(\frac{1}{2}x^2 - 3x^{-\frac{1}{2}}\right)dx$$

Integrate the left-hand side and you get y.
And you can rewrite the right-hand side to break it into smaller bits...

$$y = \frac{1}{2}\int x^2\,dx - 3\int x^{-\frac{1}{2}}\,dx$$

Integrating $\frac{dy}{dx}$ gives y.

You only need to look at the x bits, so you can put the numbers outside the integration signs.

Now just integrate both terms on the right-hand side.

Integrate each term separately...

$$y = \frac{1}{2}\int x^2\,dx - 3\int x^{-\frac{1}{2}}\,dx$$

The integration formula:
$$\int x^n\,dx = \frac{x^{n+1}}{n+1} + C$$

$$\frac{1}{2}\left(\frac{x^3}{3}\right) \quad 3\left(\frac{x^{\frac{1}{2}}}{\frac{1}{2}}\right)$$

Dividing by $\frac{1}{2}$ is the same as multiplying by 2. So this term becomes $-6x^{\frac{1}{2}}$.

$$y = \frac{x^3}{6} - 6x^{\frac{1}{2}} + C \quad \text{...and add a } \underline{\text{constant of integration}}.$$

You always have to stick in a constant of integration — you don't know what it is yet, so call it C for now.

You might wonder why there's only one constant. Since you've had to do three separate mini-integrations, shouldn't there be three constants like this?

$$y + C_1 = \frac{x^3}{6} + C_2 - 6x^{\frac{1}{2}} + C_3$$

Well yes, but rather than have three separate ones, you can just make them into one.

Let $C = -C_1 + C_2 + C_3 \Rightarrow y = \frac{x^3}{6} - 6x^{\frac{1}{2}} + C$

Paper 1 Q5 — Calculus

...and then stick in the *Values* it gives for *x* and *y*

Now you've got to find C. The question says it's got to 'pass through the point $\left(1, \frac{1}{6}\right)$.'
<u>In other words</u>: when x = 1, $y = \frac{1}{6}$. Sticking this in will give you the value of C:

Substitute x = 1 and $y = \frac{1}{6}$ in the expression for y...

$$\frac{1}{6} = \frac{1^3}{6} - \left(6 \times 1^{\frac{1}{2}}\right) + C$$

$$= \frac{1}{6} - 6 + C$$

$$\Rightarrow C = 6$$

And so the complete expression for y is...

$$y = \frac{x^3}{6} - 6x^{\frac{1}{2}} + 6$$

You should check your answer by:

(i) putting in x = 1 (and making sure you get $\frac{1}{6}$)

and (ii) differentiating it (and making sure you get the derivative in the question).

(ii) A simple *Limit Integral* — but don't fall into the *Trap*

'Evaluate $\int_0^1 y\,dx$.'

This part is pretty standard stuff —
but there's a really obvious trap at the start.
As long as you avoid that, you can't go far wrong.

The Trap:

$$\int_0^1 y\,dx = \left[\frac{y^2}{2}\right]_0^1 = \frac{1}{2} - 0 = \frac{1}{2}$$

This is rubbish! — because this is
integrating with respect to y, not x.

The Right Way:

$$\int_0^1 y\,dx.$$

The 'dx' means you're integrating <u>with respect to x</u>.
So you need to write y <u>in terms of x</u> before you integrate. (i.e. stick in the answer to part (i).)

$$\int_0^1 y\,dx = \int_0^1 \left(\frac{x^3}{6} - 6x^{\frac{1}{2}} + 6\right)dx$$

You could break this up into individual chunks like
before — but you don't have to. Do whatever's easier.

It's a limit integral, so integrate the bracket — and stick it in a big square bracket with limits.

$$\int_0^1 y\,dx = \int_0^1 \left(\frac{x^3}{6} - 6x^{\frac{1}{2}} + 6\right)dx = \left[\frac{x^4}{6 \times 4} - \frac{6x^{\frac{3}{2}}}{\frac{3}{2}} + \frac{6x^1}{1}\right]_0^1$$

$$= \left[\frac{x^4}{24} - 4x^{\frac{3}{2}} + 6x\right]_0^1$$

$\frac{6}{\frac{3}{2}} = 6 \times \frac{2}{3} = \frac{12}{3} = 4$

Now evaluate the square bracket — use the <u>top limit</u> first, then <u>subtract</u> what you get when you use the <u>bottom limit</u>.

$$\int_0^1 y\,dx = \left(\frac{1^4}{24} - \left(4 \times 1^{\frac{3}{2}}\right) + (6 \times 1)\right) - \left(\frac{0^4}{24} - \left(4 \times 0^{\frac{3}{2}}\right) + (6 \times 0)\right)$$

$$= \frac{1}{24} - 4 + 6$$

$$= \frac{49}{24}$$

When you put x = 0, all these
parts are equal to zero.

$\frac{1}{24} - 4 + 6 = \frac{1}{24} + 2 = \frac{1+48}{24} = \frac{49}{24}$

Integration — Int it great? ...no? Oh... didn't think so...

This question is a gift — it's all real standard stuff. So if you're struggling with it, bury your head in those maths books until it begins to make sense. And another thing — always make sure you use all the info the question gives you, e.g. if it says the graph passes through the point (joe, bloggs), it means "at some point in the question, you need to plug in the values x=joe when y=bloggs". And watch for that trap at the end — the 'dx' in an integral means you have to integrate x's.

Paper 1 Q6 — Arithmetic Series

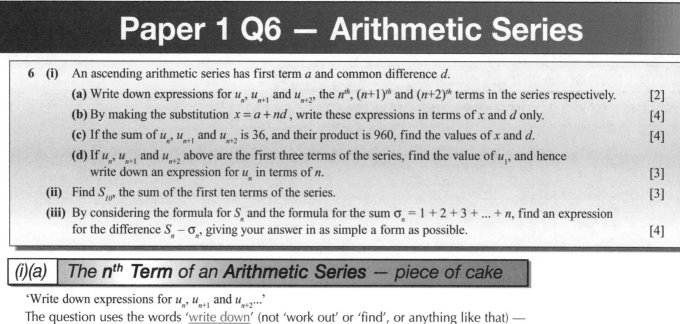

6 (i) An ascending arithmetic series has first term a and common difference d.

(a) Write down expressions for u_n, u_{n+1} and u_{n+2}, the nth, $(n+1)^{th}$ and $(n+2)^{th}$ terms in the series respectively. [2]

(b) By making the substitution $x = a + nd$, write these expressions in terms of x and d only. [4]

(c) If the sum of u_n, u_{n+1} and u_{n+2} is 36, and their product is 960, find the values of x and d. [4]

(d) If u_n, u_{n+1} and u_{n+2} above are the first three terms of the series, find the value of u_1, and hence write down an expression for u_n in terms of n. [3]

(ii) Find S_{10}, the sum of the first ten terms of the series. [3]

(iii) By considering the formula for S_n and the formula for the sum $\sigma_n = 1 + 2 + 3 + ... + n$, find an expression for the difference $S_n - \sigma_n$, giving your answer in as simple a form as possible. [4]

(i)(a) The nth Term of an Arithmetic Series — piece of cake

'Write down expressions for u_n, u_{n+1} and u_{n+2}...'
The question uses the words 'write down' (not 'work out' or 'find', or anything like that) —
so you should just be able to quote the answer without thinking about it.

For an arithmetic series, the nth term is just: $u_n = a + (n - 1)d$, so...

$$u_n = a + (n-1)d$$
$$u_{n+1} = a + nd$$
$$u_{n+2} = a + (n+1)d$$

Use the same formula each time, but substitute (n+1) and (n+2) for n.
E.g. $u_{n+1} = a + [(n + 1) - 1]d = a + nd$, etc.

(i)(b) Substitute — and then Rewrite

'By making the substitution $x = a + nd$, write these expressions in terms of x and d only.'

So you've got to rewrite those same expressions, but with only x and d on the right-hand side.
But at least it tells you how to do it — by writing x instead of 'a + nd'.

$$u_n = a + (n-1)d = a + nd - d = x - d$$
$$u_{n+1} = a + nd = x$$
$$u_{n+2} = a + (n+1)d = a + nd + d = x + d$$

Work out the brackets in the answers to part (i), and then write x wherever you see 'a+nd'.

(i)(c) Fiddle About a bit to find x and d

'If the sum of u_n, u_{n+1} and u_{n+2} is 36, and their product is 960, find the values of x and d.'

This looks hard — but there are some big clues in the question. It tells you what the <u>sum</u>
and <u>product</u> of the expressions in part (b) equal — so start by working those out...

The sum is:
$$u_n + u_{n+1} + u_{n+2} = (x-d) + x + (x+d)$$
$$= 3x$$

The <u>sum</u> of a load of numbers is what you get when you <u>add</u> them all together.

The <u>product</u> of a load of numbers is what you get when you <u>multiply</u> them all together.

And this equals 36, so...
$$3x = 36$$
$$\Rightarrow x = 12$$

The product is:
$$u_n \times u_{n+1} \times u_{n+2} = (x-d)x(x+d)$$
$$= x(x^2 - d^2)$$

Using the difference of two squares: $(x + d)(x - d) = x^2 - d^2$.

This equals 960. But you've just worked out that x = 12 — so put this value in as well...
$$x(x^2 - d^2) = 960$$
$$\Rightarrow 12(144 - d^2) = 960$$

This only has one letter left to find, d.

And now you can find the value of d...
$$\Rightarrow 144 - d^2 = 80$$

$\frac{960}{12} = 80$

$$\Rightarrow d^2 = 144 - 80 = 64$$
$$\Rightarrow d = 8$$

You need to take the positive square root to get d, because the question tells you the series is ascending.

Paper 1 Q6 — Arithmetic Series

(i)(d) | Now find the **First Term** using your answers from before...

'...find the value of u_1, and hence write down an expression for u_n in terms of n.'

If u_n, u_{n+1} and u_{n+2} are the first three terms of the series, then

$$u_1 = u_n = x - d = 12 - 8 = 4$$

Using your answers from parts (b) and (c).

...which means the nth term of the series is:

$$u_n = a + (n-1)d = 4 + 8(n-1)$$
$$= 4 + 8n - 8 = 8n - 4$$

You've just worked out that the first term of the series u_1 (= a) is 4.

(ii) | **Sum** an arithmetic series

'Find S_{10}, the sum of the first ten terms of the series.'

This is an absolute doddle — as long as you know the formula for the sum of the first n terms of an arithmetic series...

The formula for the sum of the first n terms of an arithmetic series is:

$$S_n = \frac{n}{2}[2a + (n-1)d]$$

This is the general formula for the sum of the first n terms...

Or you can use the other formula for the sum of the first n terms of an arithmetic series: $S_n = \frac{n}{2}(a+l)$.

And so if n = 10:

$$S_{10} = 5[2a + 9d]$$

...so if you only want the sum of the first ten terms, use this one.

Putting in the values of a (= 4) and d (= 8), you get...

$$S_{10} = 5[(2 \times 4) + (9 \times 8)]$$
$$= 5 \times 80 = 400$$

(iii) | What do the examiners want now — Blood...

'...find an expression for the difference $S_n - \sigma_n$...'

Right then — now it's serious. This bit looks nasty — but just do it one bit at a time.

You've already got the formula for S_n. It is:

$$S_n = \frac{n}{2}[2a + (n-1)d]$$

And since you know a = 4 and d = 8, this becomes:

$$S_n = \frac{n}{2}[8 + 8(n-1)]$$
$$= \frac{n}{2}[8 + 8n - 8]$$
$$= \frac{n}{2}(8n) = 4n^2$$

Now $\sigma_n = 1 + 2 + 3 + ... + n$, and you should know that this sum is given by:

$$\sigma_n = 1 + 2 + ... + n = \sum_{i=1}^{n} i = \frac{n}{2}(n+1)$$

You'll need to remember this formula.

And all the question's actually asking you to do is work out $S_n - \sigma_n$. This is just:

$$S_n - \sigma_n = 4n^2 - \frac{n}{2}(n+1)$$
$$= 4n^2 - \frac{n^2}{2} - \frac{n}{2}$$
$$= \frac{7}{2}n^2 - \frac{n}{2}$$
$$= \frac{n}{2}(7n - 1)$$

Taking a factor of $\frac{n}{2}$ outside the brackets.

Check your answer: choose n = 3.
$S_3 = 4 + 12 + 20 = 36$.
$\sigma_3 = 1 + 2 + 3 = 6$.
According to your formula the difference between them should be: $\frac{3}{2}((7 \times 3) - 1) = 30$. And since $36 - 6 = 30$, this works.

When the question says jump — you ask, 'How high...'

A lot of questions look mean, but when you get past the 'maths-speak' they're not really so bad. When they give 'advice' on tackling a problem, it's a good idea to take it — do as you're told, basically. Also, with this question (like a load of others), you can check your answer by choosing a (small) value for n and seeing if your formula works. Then if it does work, you can do the next question with a warm happy feeling inside. Wonderful...

Paper 1 Q7 — Logs and Exponentials

7 (i) (a) Show that $\log_3 9 = 2$ [1]

      (b) Find the value of $\log_3 (9^3)$ [2]

      (c) Find the value of $\log_3 \dfrac{1}{\sqrt[3]{9}}$ [3]

   (ii) Solve:

      (a) $\log_2 x = 7$ [1]

      (b) $10^{4x} = 300$ [2]

      (c) $6^x = 40$ [3]

(i)(a)   A nice easy one to start with...

'Show that $\log_3 9 = 2$'

The question is testing whether you know the very basics about logs.
All you need to know is that '$\log_3 9$' means '**the power you have to raise 3 to, to get 9**'.

You know that: $3^2 = 9$

so: $\log_3 9 = 2$

Always remember that the answers you get at the start of a question will probably be useful for tackling the rest of the question.

(i)(b)   It's a bit like part (a) — but with an extra power of 3

'Find the value of $\log_3 (9^3)$'

Use the laws of logs to sort this out.

You know that: $\log_a (x^k) = k \log_a x$

so: $\log_3 (9^3) = 3 \, \boxed{\log_3 9}$

$= 3 \times \boxed{2}$

$= 6$

This is what you worked out for (i)(a).

Laws of Logarithms

$$\log_a x + \log_a y = \log_a (xy)$$

$$\log_a x - \log_a y = \log_a \left(\frac{x}{y}\right)$$

$$\log_a (x^k) = k \log_a x$$

You'll need to know these laws for questions on logs. It's definitely a good idea to learn them.

(i)(c)   Write the Cube Root as a Power and use Laws of Logs again

'Find the value of $\log_3 \dfrac{1}{\sqrt[3]{9}}$'

Powers are often easier to work with than roots and fractions:

$$\frac{1}{\sqrt[3]{9}} = \frac{1}{9^{1/3}} = 9^{-\frac{1}{3}}$$

$\sqrt[x]{a} = a^{\frac{1}{x}}$ $\dfrac{1}{a^x} = a^{-x}$

Make use of the power rules.

Now use the law of logs you used earlier:

$$\log_3 9^{-\frac{1}{3}} = -\frac{1}{3} \log_3 9$$

$$= -\frac{1}{3} \times 2 = -\frac{2}{3}$$

Paper 1 Q7 — Logs and Exponentials

(ii)(a) | To Solve Equations you need x on its own

'Solve: $\log_2 x = 7$'

This looks a bit tricky — but have a look back at (i)(a) for a few clues.

Putting the equation into words, you get '7 is the power you raise 2 to, to get x'.

In other words: $x = 2^7 = 128$

(ii)(b) | Use Logs to bring Powers down (otherwise they'll bring you down) | ...urghhh

'Solve: $10^{4x} = 300$'

You need to tackle the left-hand side of this equation because that's where the 'x' is lurking.

You'll need to take logs to the base 10, which will leave you with: $\log_{10} 10^{4x} = \log_{10} 300$

You can simplify the LHS by asking yourself:

'10 raised to the power of what equals 10^{4x}?'

Clearly that's just 4x: $4x = \log_{10} 300$

Now x is safely at ground level, the rest is easy: $x = \dfrac{\log_{10} 300}{4} = 0.619$ (3 s.f.)

(ii)(c) | This time the base of the power is 6, not 10

'Solve: $6^x = 40$'

You don't have a button on your calculator that does $\log_6$, so start by taking logs to the base 10 again.

$$\log_{10}(6^x) = \log_{10} 40$$

Use the law of logs on the LHS: $x \log_{10} 6 = \log_{10} 40$ ⟶ This is the rule you use: $\log_a(x^k) = k \log_a x$

Putting these two equations together you get: $x = \dfrac{\log_{10} 40}{\log_{10} 6}$

$$= \frac{1.602}{0.778}$$

$$= 2.06 \text{ (3 s.f.)}$$

There's a very small cow at the end of the index... *she's called Bob.*

I don't want to be accused of, you know, *labouring* a point — but *LEARN THE POWER LAWS,* and while you're at it *LEARN THE LOG LAWS.* If you don't know the rules, you can't answer the questions — it's *that* simple. Here endeth the lesson.

Anyway, moving on — you might have noticed the distinct lack of 'log' puns on this page.
I can sense your disappointment. So just for you, here are a few that didn't quite make it...

"Hit me baby one more log..." (one of the more surreal offerings), *"Logs — the cheap and easy alternative pet..."*
(bit of a Twin Peaks reference, never mind), *"A log, log time ago, I can still remember, how exponentials used to make me smile...", "Logs — just burn 'em...", "Where can you look if you need a new logarithm — a cata-log...", "What do you call a log talking to itself — a mono-log...", "Captain's Log, stardate...* I'll just stop there shall I...

Paper 1 Q8 — Sector Areas

8 The diagram below shows a sector of a circle of radius *r* cm and angle 120°.
   The length of the arc of the sector is 40 cm.

   (i) Write 120° in radians.   [1]

   (ii) Show that *r* ≈ 19.1 cm.   [2]

   (iii) Find the area of the sector to the nearest square centimetre.   [3]

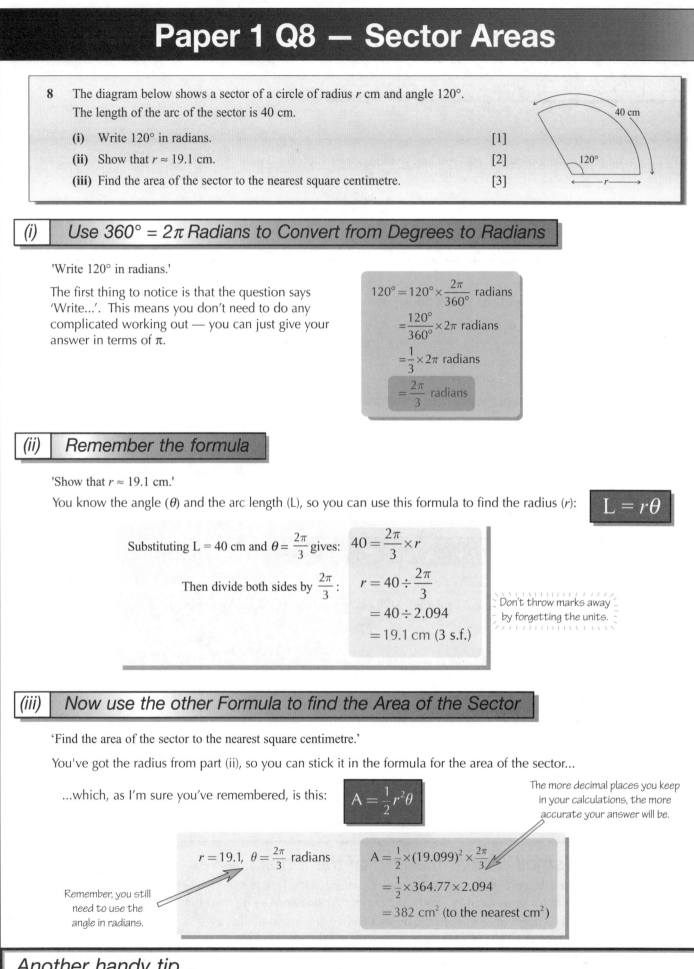

(i) *Use 360° = 2π Radians to Convert from Degrees to Radians*

'Write 120° in radians.'

The first thing to notice is that the question says 'Write...'. This means you don't need to do any complicated working out — you can just give your answer in terms of π.

$$120° = 120° \times \frac{2\pi}{360°} \text{ radians}$$
$$= \frac{120°}{360°} \times 2\pi \text{ radians}$$
$$= \frac{1}{3} \times 2\pi \text{ radians}$$
$$= \frac{2\pi}{3} \text{ radians}$$

(ii) *Remember the formula*

'Show that *r* ≈ 19.1 cm.'

You know the angle (θ) and the arc length (L), so you can use this formula to find the radius (*r*): $$L = r\theta$$

Substituting L = 40 cm and $\theta = \frac{2\pi}{3}$ gives: $$40 = \frac{2\pi}{3} \times r$$

Then divide both sides by $\frac{2\pi}{3}$: $$r = 40 \div \frac{2\pi}{3}$$
$$= 40 \div 2.094$$
$$= 19.1 \text{ cm (3 s.f.)}$$

Don't throw marks away by forgetting the units.

(iii) *Now use the other Formula to find the Area of the Sector*

'Find the area of the sector to the nearest square centimetre.'

You've got the radius from part (ii), so you can stick it in the formula for the area of the sector...

...which, as I'm sure you've remembered, is this: $$A = \frac{1}{2}r^2\theta$$

The more decimal places you keep in your calculations, the more accurate your answer will be.

$r = 19.1$, $\theta = \frac{2\pi}{3}$ radians

Remember, you still need to use the angle in radians.

$$A = \frac{1}{2} \times (19.099)^2 \times \frac{2\pi}{3}$$
$$= \frac{1}{2} \times 364.77 \times 2.094$$
$$= 382 \text{ cm}^2 \text{ (to the nearest cm}^2)$$

Another handy tip...

If you're not sure if you've remembered the area formula properly, put in 2π for θ and make sure it gives you πr^2, because 2π = 360° = a full circle.   Alternatively, of course, you can just learn them, which might be easier.

General Certificate of Education
Advanced Subsidiary (AS) and Advanced Level

Core 2 Mathematics — Practice Exam Two

Give non-exact numerical answers correct to 3 significant figures, unless a
different degree of accuracy is specified in the question or is clearly appropriate.

1 **(i)** Rewrite the following expression in the form $f(x) = 0$, where $f(x)$ is of the form $f(x) = ax^2 + bx + c$.
$$(x-1)(x-4) = 2x^2 + 11$$ [2]

(ii) By completing the square, or otherwise, show that $f(x) = 0$ has no roots. [3]

(iii) Sketch the graph of $f(x)$. Evaluate the area enclosed by the graph of $f(x)$, the line $y = \dfrac{1}{\sqrt{2}}$,
the line $x = \sqrt{2}$ and the y-axis. [4]

2 **(i)** Sketch the graph of $y = \cos(x - 60°)$ for x between $0°$ and $360°$. [3]

(ii) Show that the equation
$$2\sin^2(x - 60°) = 1 + \cos(x - 60°)$$ may be written as a quadratic in $\cos(x - 60°)$. [4]

(iii) Hence solve this equation, giving all values of x such that $0° \le x \le 360°$. [4]

3 **(i)** Write down the first four terms in the expansion of $(1 + ax)^{10}$, $a > 0$. [2]

(ii) Find the coefficient of x^2 in the expansion of $(2 + 3x)^5$. [2]

(iii) If the coefficients of x^2 in both expansions are equal, find the value of a. [3]

4 **(i)** Find the missing length a in the triangle. [4]

(ii) Find the angles θ and ϕ. [4]

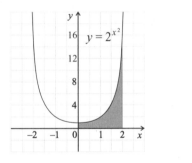

5 The diagram shows the graph of $y = 2^{x^2}$.

(i) Use the trapezium rule with 4 intervals to find an estimate for the
area of the region bounded by the axes, the curve and the line x = 2. [4]

(ii) State whether the estimate in (i) is an overestimate or
an underestimate, giving a reason for your answer. [2]

6 **(i)** **(a)** Show that the graph of $f(x) = -x^2(x - 2)$ has turning points at the origin and the point $\left(\dfrac{4}{3}, \dfrac{32}{27}\right)$. [3]

(b) Sketch the graph of $f(x)$, marking in any turning points and points where it crosses the axes. [2]

(ii) The function $g(x)$ is defined by $g(x) = 2 - x$. Given that the graphs of $f(x)$ and $g(x)$ meet at $x = 1$,
sketch the graph of $g(x)$ on the same set of axes you used in part (i), marking in the coordinates of the two
points of intersection for which x is positive. [3]

(iii) Show that the area enclosed by the two graphs between $x = 1$ and $x = 2$ is $\dfrac{5}{12}$. [4]

7 **(i)** Sketch the graph of $y = 1 - (x - 2)^2$, marking carefully the points where the curve meets the coordinate axes. [3]

(ii) Using the same axes, sketch the graph of $y = 1.5x - 2$. [2]

(iii) Prove that the x-coordinates of the points of intersection of the two graphs satisfy the equation $2x^2 - 5x + 2 = 0$. [3]

(iv) Solve this equation to find the coordinates of the points of intersection of the two graphs. [3]

8 For the series with second term –2 and common ratio –½, find:

(i) the first term [2]

(ii) the first seven terms [3]

(iii) the sum of the first seven terms [3]

(iv) the sum to infinity [3]

Paper 2 Q1 — Graphs and Integration

1 **(i)** Rewrite the following expression in the form $f(x) = 0$, where $f(x)$ is of the form $f(x) = ax^2 + bx + c$.

$$(x-1)(x-4) = 2x^2 + 11$$ [2]

(ii) By completing the square, or otherwise, show that $f(x) = 0$ has no roots. [3]

(iii) Sketch the graph of $f(x)$. Evaluate the area enclosed by the graph of $f(x)$, the line $y = \frac{1}{\sqrt{2}}$,

the line $x = \sqrt{2}$ and the y-axis. [4]

(i) | The first part's *Really Simple*

'Rewrite the following expression in the form $f(x) = 0$, where f(x) is of the form $f(x) = ax^2 + bx + c$.'
$$(x-1)(x-4) = 2x^2 + 11$$

The first thing to do is get rid of the brackets. So multiply them out:

$$x^2 - 5x + 4 = 2x^2 + 11$$

And rearrange, putting everything on one side (you want zero on the right-hand side).

$$-x^2 - 5x - 7 = 0$$
$$\Rightarrow x^2 + 5x + 7 = 0$$

And that's part (i) done. (So a=1, b=5, and c=7.)

(ii) | *Complete* the Square and *Use* it

'By completing the square, or otherwise, show that $f(x) = 0$ has no roots.'

So f(x) = x²+5x+7 from part (i). The <u>question</u> says to complete the square, so let's not argue.

Write the squared bracket down with d added.

$$\left(x + \tfrac{5}{2}\right)^2 + d \longleftarrow \text{d is some unknown number.}$$

The bracket is <u>always</u>:
$$a\left(x + \frac{b}{2a}\right)^2$$

You need to find a value for d such that $\left(x + \tfrac{5}{2}\right)^2 + d = f(x)$

So put in the old expression for f(x):

$$\left(x + \tfrac{5}{2}\right)^2 + d = x^2 + 5x + 7$$

<u>Always</u> put:
bracket² + number = old expression for f(x).

and solve it to find d...

$$x^2 + 5x + \tfrac{25}{4} + d = x^2 + 5x + 7$$
$$d = 7 - \tfrac{25}{4} = \tfrac{3}{4}$$

The x² and x terms are the same on both sides so they cancel out. If they don't, you've got the bracket wrong.

So f(x) written in completed square form is:

$$f(x) = \left(x + \tfrac{5}{2}\right)^2 + \tfrac{3}{4}$$

You'll need to write something like this to show that you understand why it has no roots. Otherwise you won't get the marks.

You need to show that f(x)=0 has no roots.

$$f(x) = \left(x + \tfrac{5}{2}\right)^2 + \tfrac{3}{4} = 0$$

The squared bracket can <u>never</u> be less than 0. So the left-hand side can never be less than $\tfrac{3}{4}$. (So it can never be 0.) Therefore f(x) has <u>no roots</u>.

Paper 2 Q1 — Graphs and Integration

(iii) | Sketching the **Graph** of y=f(x) — use the **Completed Square**

'Sketch the graph of f(x).' $f(x) = x^2 + 5x + 7 \implies y = x^2 + 5x + 7$

To draw the graph you need to know where it has max/min points and where it crosses the axes.

The coefficient of x^2 is <u>positive</u> (it's actually 1), so it's going to be a <u>u-shaped</u> graph (rather than n-shaped).

Find where the min occurs (use the completed square form):

$$f(x) = y = \left(x + \tfrac{5}{2}\right)^2 + \tfrac{3}{4}$$

The minimum of f(x) is when the squared bracket is 0.

So 3/4 is the minimum value, and occurs when x=−5/2.

<u>Where does it cross the axes?</u>

It's <u>not</u> going to cross the x-axis, because its minimum value is ¾.
We can find where it crosses the y-axis by putting x=0:

$$x = 0 \implies y = 7$$

Evaluate the **Area** — Use Your **Sketch**

'Evaluate the area enclosed by the graph of f(x), the line $y = \frac{1}{\sqrt{2}}$, the line $x = \sqrt{2}$ and the y-axis.'

The first thing to do is to sketch the situation so you can see <u>exactly</u> what you've got to do.

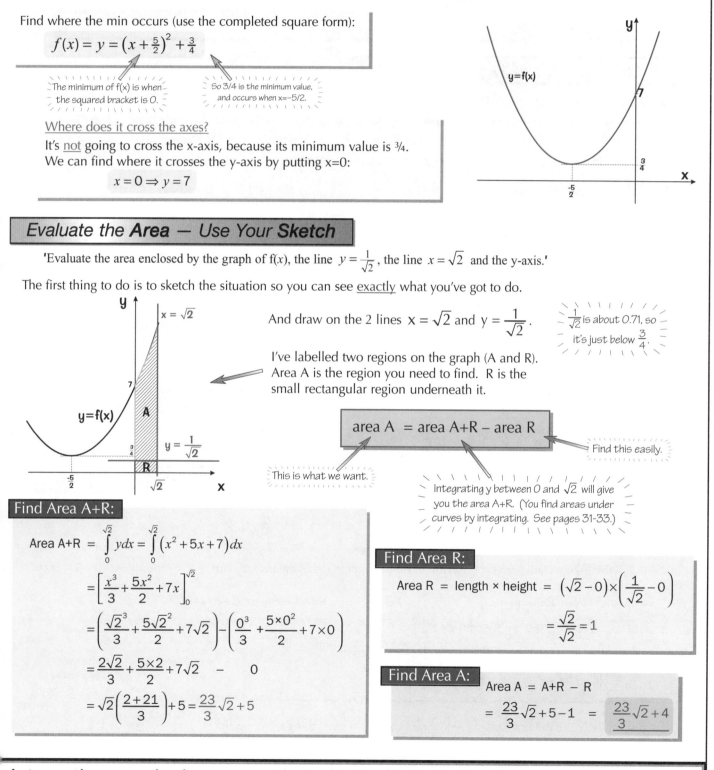

And draw on the 2 lines $x = \sqrt{2}$ and $y = \frac{1}{\sqrt{2}}$.

$\frac{1}{\sqrt{2}}$ is about 0.71, so it's just below $\frac{3}{4}$.

I've labelled two regions on the graph (A and R). Area A is the region you need to find. R is the small rectangular region underneath it.

$$\boxed{\text{area A} = \text{area A+R} - \text{area R}}$$

Find this easily.

This is what we want.

Integrating y between 0 and $\sqrt{2}$ will give you the area A+R. (You find areas under curves by integrating. See pages 31-33.)

Find Area A+R:

$$\text{Area A+R} = \int_0^{\sqrt{2}} y\,dx = \int_0^{\sqrt{2}} \left(x^2 + 5x + 7\right)dx$$

$$= \left[\frac{x^3}{3} + \frac{5x^2}{2} + 7x\right]_0^{\sqrt{2}}$$

$$= \left(\frac{\sqrt{2}^3}{3} + \frac{5\sqrt{2}^2}{2} + 7\sqrt{2}\right) - \left(\frac{0^3}{3} + \frac{5 \times 0^2}{2} + 7 \times 0\right)$$

$$= \frac{2\sqrt{2}}{3} + \frac{5 \times 2}{2} + 7\sqrt{2} \quad - \quad 0$$

$$= \sqrt{2}\left(\frac{2+21}{3}\right) + 5 = \frac{23}{3}\sqrt{2} + 5$$

Find Area R:

$$\text{Area R} = \text{length} \times \text{height} = \left(\sqrt{2} - 0\right) \times \left(\frac{1}{\sqrt{2}} - 0\right)$$

$$= \frac{\sqrt{2}}{\sqrt{2}} = 1$$

Find Area A:

$$\text{Area A} = \text{A+R} - \text{R}$$

$$= \frac{23}{3}\sqrt{2} + 5 - 1 = \frac{23}{3}\sqrt{2} + 4$$

Integrating graphs is an area that needs a lot of attention...

This is a pretty easy question, except for the last bit — and that's not <u>too</u> bad, once you've done the sketch. But if you've any sense, you'll check your answer... won't you. Your best bet with odd areas is to approximate it to easy shapes and check it's <u>about right</u>. For this question, it'd be a rectangle $\sqrt{2}$ by $\left(7 - \frac{1}{\sqrt{2}}\right)$ and a triangle $\sqrt{2}$ wide and roughly (16−7) tall.

Paper 2 Q2 — Trigonometry

2 (i) Sketch the graph of $y = \cos(x - 60°)$ for x between $0°$ and $360°$.   [3]

(ii) Show that the equation $2\sin^2(x - 60°) = 1 + \cos(x - 60°)$
may be written as a quadratic in $\cos(x - 60°)$.   [4]

(iii) Hence solve this equation, giving all values of x such that $0° \le x \le 360°$.   [4]

(i) A *cos* graph shifted 60° to the *Right*

'Sketch the graph of $y = \cos(x - 60°)$ for x between $0°$ and $360°$.'

It's pretty easy to remember that you have to shift the graph <u>sideways</u> when the '–60°' is <u>inside</u> the brackets.
But what's not so easy is to remember which <u>direction</u> to shift it — to the <u>left</u> or to the <u>right</u>.

It'll help you decide which way to move the graph if you remember this:

$\cos x = 1$ when $x = 0$.
So $\cos(x - 60°) = 1$ when $x - 60° = 0$ — and this is when <u>$x = 60°$</u>.

The graph is shifted horizontally by 60°. Because it's <u>minus</u> 60°, it's shifted to the <u>right</u>.

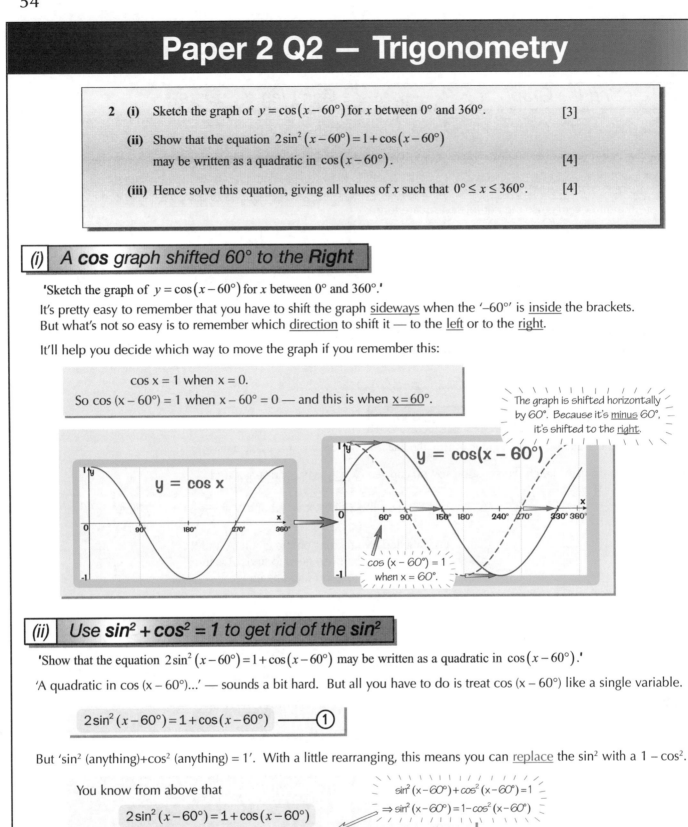

$\cos(x - 60°) = 1$ when $x = 60°$.

(ii) Use *sin²* + *cos²* = 1 to get rid of the *sin²*

'Show that the equation $2\sin^2(x - 60°) = 1 + \cos(x - 60°)$ may be written as a quadratic in $\cos(x - 60°)$.'

'A quadratic in $\cos(x - 60°)$...' — sounds a bit hard. But all you have to do is treat $\cos(x - 60°)$ like a single variable.

$$2\sin^2(x - 60°) = 1 + \cos(x - 60°) \quad\text{———①}$$

But '$\sin^2(\text{anything}) + \cos^2(\text{anything}) = 1$'. With a little rearranging, this means you can <u>replace</u> the $\sin^2$ with a $1 - \cos^2$.

You know from above that

$$2\sin^2(x - 60°) = 1 + \cos(x - 60°)$$

$\sin^2(x - 60°) + \cos^2(x - 60°) = 1$
$\Rightarrow \sin^2(x - 60°) = 1 - \cos^2(x - 60°)$

Now you can substitute for $\sin^2(x - 60°)$ in this to give...

$$2\{1 - \cos^2(x - 60°)\} = 1 + \cos(x - 60°)$$

You could even substitute y for x–60° — and work with sin²y and cos²y instead.

Now just multiply out the bracket and <u>rearrange</u> this so that everything's on one side.

$$2\{1 - \cos^2(x - 60°)\} = 1 + \cos(x - 60°)$$
$$\Rightarrow 2 - 2\cos^2(x - 60°) = 1 + \cos(x - 60°)$$
$$\Rightarrow 2\cos^2(x - 60°) + \cos(x - 60°) - 1 = 0$$

If you write y = cos(x – 60°), then this is $2y^2 + y - 1 = 0$. That's what the question means by 'a quadratic in cos(x – 60°)'.

Paper 2 Q2 — Trigonometry

(iii) It's a **Quadratic**, so try to **Factorise** it

'Hence solve this equation, giving all values of x such that $0° \leq x \leq 360°$.'

It's another question that looks a lot more frightening than it actually is. The most important thing is that you do it one bit at a time. You've got a quadratic equation (even though it's a horrible-looking one), so try to factorise it.

But it's probably a good idea to <u>rewrite</u> it a bit first so that it looks friendlier...

$$2\cos^2(x-60°) + \cos(x-60°) - 1 = 0$$

If you substitute y for cos(x – 60°), this becomes...

$$2y^2 + y - 1 = 0$$

Yep, it's a normal quadratic, so try to factorise it — and if it won't factorise, use the quadratic formula.

This quadratic factorises to give...

$$(2y-1)(y+1) = 0$$
$$\Rightarrow y = \tfrac{1}{2} \quad \text{or} \quad y = -1$$

So you've found what y is. But y = cos(x – 60°), and so...

$$\cos(x-60°) = \tfrac{1}{2} \quad \text{or} \quad \cos(x-60°) = -1$$

At this stage, alarm bells should definitely be ringing — you've just drawn the graph of y = cos(x – 60°), and you can use that to help solve this part.

And by taking the inverse cosine of these, you get...

$$x - 60° = \cos^{-1}\left(\tfrac{1}{2}\right) = 60°$$
$$\Rightarrow x = 120°$$

or

$$x - 60° = \cos^{-1}(-1) = 180°$$
$$\Rightarrow x = 240°$$

Get these values from your calculator.

So far, you've got two solutions — but there might be <u>more</u>. It's time to have another look at the graph from part 1. That's basically why they asked you to draw it — to <u>help</u> you with this part.

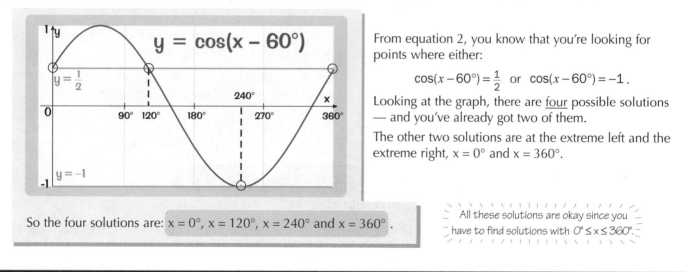

From equation 2, you know that you're looking for points where either:

$$\cos(x-60°) = \tfrac{1}{2} \quad \text{or} \quad \cos(x-60°) = -1 .$$

Looking at the graph, there are <u>four</u> possible solutions — and you've already got two of them.

The other two solutions are at the extreme left and the extreme right, x = 0° and x = 360°.

So the four solutions are: x = 0°, x = 120°, x = 240° and x = 360°.

All these solutions are okay since you have to find solutions with $0° \leq x \leq 360°$.

Get a tan — cos you're worth it...

What a question — what a pain. It relies on knowing all sorts of things: graphs, sin² + cos² = 1, solving quadratics, solving trig equations, and more besides. The thing to remember, though, is that with questions like this, later parts often make use of stuff you worked out in the earlier sections — so if something seems outrageously difficult, have a look at what you've already done and see if you can get a hint from that.

Paper 2 Q3 — Binomial Expansion

> 3 (i) Write down the first four terms in the expansion of $(1 + ax)^{10}$, $a > 0$. [2]
>
> (ii) Find the coefficient of x^2 in the expansion of $(2 + 3x)^5$. [2]
>
> (iii) If the coefficients of x^2 in both expansions are equal, find the value of a. [3]

(i) Binomial Expansion — Use the Formula but watch out for the 'a'

'Write down the first four terms in the expansion of $(1 + ax)^{10}$, $a > 0$.'

It's a binomial expansion. That means you have two choices: Pascal's Triangle or the formula.

Now you *could* use Pascal's triangle — but it's a very high power, so it'd take you half the exam and leave you with no room to answer the question. So it's time to dig out the formula. (If you don't know this by now — learn it.)

(1) Start by writing down the formula:

$$(1+x)^n = 1 + \frac{n}{1}x + \frac{n(n-1)}{1\times 2}x^2 + \frac{n(n-1)(n-2)}{1\times 2\times 3}x^3 + \ldots + \ldots + x^n$$

(2) Then write out the expression from the question...

$$(1 + ax)^{10}$$

Before you go any further, alarm bells should be ringing — you've got 'ax' instead of 'x'. Just remember that, OK.

(3) ...expand it...

REMEMBER — square / cube the WHOLE BRACKET, not just the 'x'.

$$= 1 + \frac{10}{1}(ax) + \frac{10\times 9}{1\times 2}(ax)^2 + \frac{10\times 9\times 8}{1\times 2\times 3}(ax)^3 + \ldots$$

(4) ...and finally, simplify it.

$$= 1 + 10ax + \frac{90}{2}a^2x^2 + \frac{720}{6}a^3x^3 + \ldots$$

$$= 1 + 10ax + 45a^2x^2 + 120a^3x^3 + \ldots$$

(ii) Binomial Expansion again — Watch out for the '2'

'Find the coefficient of x^2 in the expansion of $(2 + 3x)^5$.'

(1) Again — start by writing down the formula:

$$(1+x)^n = 1 + \frac{n}{1}x + \frac{n(n-1)}{1\times 2}x^2 + \frac{n(n-1)(n-2)}{1\times 2\times 3}x^3 + \ldots + \ldots + x^n$$

(2) Then write out the expression from the question...

$$(2 + 3x)^5$$

Again, look out. This time you've got a '2', not a '1', and you've got a '3x' instead of an 'x'.,

(3) Take a factor of 2 out to get it in the form you want:

$$(2+3x)^5 = \left[2(1+\tfrac{3}{2}x)\right]^5$$

Remember to take the 2 to the power of 5, not just the bracket.

$$= 2^5(1+\tfrac{3}{2}x)^5$$

$$= 32(1+\tfrac{3}{2}x)^5$$

(4) Then expand it as before (only up to the x^2 term):

$$32(1+\tfrac{3}{2}x)^5 = 32\left[1 + \frac{5}{1}(\tfrac{3}{2}x) + \frac{5\times 4}{1\times 2}(\tfrac{3}{2}x)^2 + \ldots\right]$$

(5) You only need the x^2 term so just simplify that one:

Cancel as much as you can to make the calculation easier.

$$x^2 \text{ term} = 32\times\frac{5\times 4}{1\times 2}(\tfrac{3}{2}x)^2$$

$$= \frac{\overset{16}{\cancel{32}}\times\overset{5}{\cancel{20}}}{1}\times\frac{9}{\cancel{4}_{1}}x^2 = 16\times 5\times 9x^2 = 80\times 9x^2 = 720x^2$$

(iii) Equate coefficients from the first two answers — no problem

'If the coefficients of x^2 in both expansions are equal, find the value of a.'

You're told that the coefficients in the terms (i) $45a^2x^2$ and (ii) $720x^2$ are equal, so . . . put them equal to each other!

(genius)

$$45a^2 = 720 \implies a = \pm\sqrt{\frac{720}{45}} = \pm\sqrt{16} = \pm 4$$

But since it says in Question (i) that $a > 0$, you can confidently say that $a = 4$.

binomial expansion: $(1 + \text{binomial})^7 = 1 + 7\,\text{binomial} + 21\,\text{binomial}^2 + 35\,\text{binomial}^3 + \ldots$ ho ho

The problem with the binomial expansion is that it's a bit fiddly — there are loads of bits to it, and that means loads of opportunities for mucking it up. So the best advice is to *LEARN* the expansion and use it very, very *CAREFULLY*.

Paper 2 Q4 — Sine and Cosine Rules

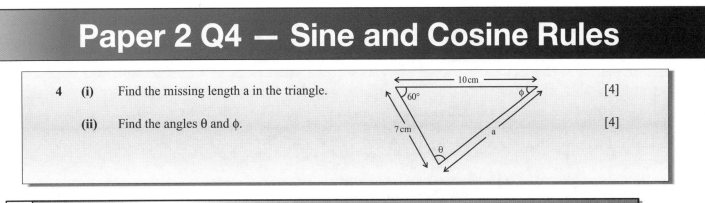

4 **(i)** Find the missing length a in the triangle. [4]

(ii) Find the angles θ and φ. [4]

(i) *If you only know an Angle and the Sides next to it, use the Cosine Rule*

'Find the missing length a...'

If you're asked to find a side or angle of a triangle without a right angle, there are two things you can try — the <u>Sine Rule</u> and the <u>Cosine Rule</u>. But to use the Sine Rule, you need to know both an angle and the length of the side opposite it. If you don't (like here), it'll have to be the Cosine Rule.

Use the Cosine Rule: $a^2 = b^2 + c^2 - 2bc \cos A$, putting b=10, c=7 and the angle A=60°.

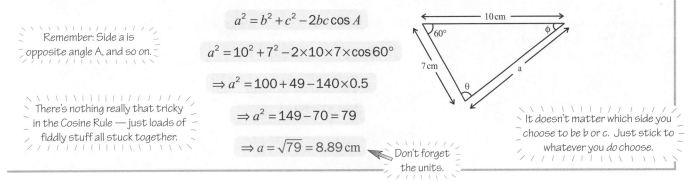

$$a^2 = b^2 + c^2 - 2bc \cos A$$

$$a^2 = 10^2 + 7^2 - 2 \times 10 \times 7 \times \cos 60°$$

$$\Rightarrow a^2 = 100 + 49 - 140 \times 0.5$$

$$\Rightarrow a^2 = 149 - 70 = 79$$

$$\Rightarrow a = \sqrt{79} = 8.89 \text{ cm}$$

Remember: Side a is opposite angle A, and so on.

There's nothing really that tricky in the Cosine Rule — just loads of fiddly stuff all stuck together.

Don't forget the units.

It doesn't matter which side you choose to be b or c. Just stick to whatever you do choose.

(ii) *Use the Sine Rule to find the missing angles*

You've found side a in the first part of the question — so you know an angle and the length of the side opposite. Time to use the <u>Sine Rule</u> then. Don't worry — it's easier than falling off a watermelon.

'Find the angles θ...'

Now θ is the angle opposite the 10 cm side, and I called the 10 cm side b. So in the Sine Rule, θ is the angle B.

Put the values you know into the Sine Rule.

$$\frac{a}{\sin A} = \frac{b}{\sin B}$$

$$\frac{\sqrt{79}}{\sin 60°} = \frac{10}{\sin B}$$

Take sin B over to the left, and everything else to the right.

$$\Rightarrow \sin B = \frac{10 \times \sin 60°}{\sqrt{79}} = 0.974$$

$$\Rightarrow B = \sin^{-1} 0.9744 = 77.0°$$

The <u>Sine Rule</u>: In <u>any</u> triangle,

$$\frac{a}{\sin A} = \frac{b}{\sin B} = \frac{c}{\sin C}$$

The <u>Cosine Rule</u>: In <u>any</u> triangle,

$$a^2 = b^2 + c^2 - 2bc \cos A$$

'...and φ.'

Do exactly what you've just done. But use side c instead of b.

Put the values you know into the sine rule.

$$\frac{a}{\sin A} = \frac{c}{\sin C}$$

Rearrange things a bit.

And again — take the inverse sine to find the angle.

$$\Rightarrow \sin C = \frac{7 \times \sin 60°}{\sqrt{79}} = 0.6820$$

$$\Rightarrow C = \sin^{-1} 0.6820 = 43.0°$$

(Or you could just subtract the 2 angles you know from 180° — which is a good check.)

Try to keep the full decimal answers on your calculator throughout the calculation. You should only actually round your answer at the very end.

The Sine and Cosine Rules — I know what you're thinking...

The Sine and Cosine Rules are pretty darn easy, let's face it. If you get a question in the exam on them, you should be jumping for joy. They're both really flexible — for a triangle ABC, you could use any of these for the Cosine Rule: $a^2 = b^2 + c^2 - 2bc \cos A$, $b^2 = a^2 + c^2 - 2ac \cos B$, $c^2 = a^2 + b^2 - 2ab \cos C$. And for the Sine Rule, you can <u>either</u> put the lengths or the sine bits on the top:

So either write it $\frac{a}{\sin A} = \frac{b}{\sin B} = \frac{c}{\sin C}$ or $\frac{\sin A}{a} = \frac{\sin B}{b} = \frac{\sin C}{c}$. Wow!

Paper 2 Q5 — Trapezium Rule

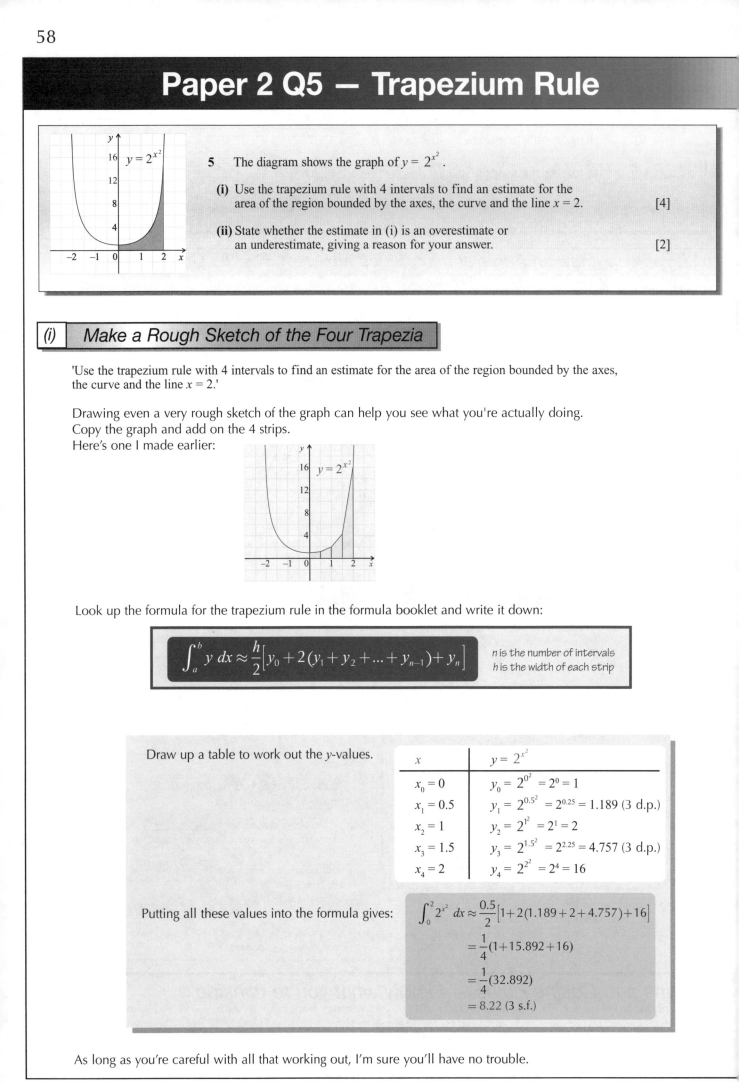

5 The diagram shows the graph of $y = 2^{x^2}$.

(i) Use the trapezium rule with 4 intervals to find an estimate for the area of the region bounded by the axes, the curve and the line $x = 2$. [4]

(ii) State whether the estimate in (i) is an overestimate or an underestimate, giving a reason for your answer. [2]

(i) | *Make a Rough Sketch of the Four Trapezia*

'Use the trapezium rule with 4 intervals to find an estimate for the area of the region bounded by the axes, the curve and the line $x = 2$.'

Drawing even a very rough sketch of the graph can help you see what you're actually doing.
Copy the graph and add on the 4 strips.
Here's one I made earlier:

Look up the formula for the trapezium rule in the formula booklet and write it down:

$$\int_a^b y \, dx \approx \frac{h}{2}\left[y_0 + 2(y_1 + y_2 + \ldots + y_{n-1}) + y_n\right]$$

n is the number of intervals
h is the width of each strip

Draw up a table to work out the *y*-values.

x	$y = 2^{x^2}$
$x_0 = 0$	$y_0 = 2^{0^2} = 2^0 = 1$
$x_1 = 0.5$	$y_1 = 2^{0.5^2} = 2^{0.25} = 1.189$ (3 d.p.)
$x_2 = 1$	$y_2 = 2^{1^2} = 2^1 = 2$
$x_3 = 1.5$	$y_3 = 2^{1.5^2} = 2^{2.25} = 4.757$ (3 d.p.)
$x_4 = 2$	$y_4 = 2^{2^2} = 2^4 = 16$

Putting all these values into the formula gives:

$$\int_0^2 2^{x^2} \, dx \approx \frac{0.5}{2}\left[1 + 2(1.189 + 2 + 4.757) + 16\right]$$

$$= \frac{1}{4}(1 + 15.892 + 16)$$

$$= \frac{1}{4}(32.892)$$

$$= 8.22 \text{ (3 s.f.)}$$

As long as you're careful with all that working out, I'm sure you'll have no trouble.

Paper 2 Q5 — Trapezium Rule

(ii) *The shape of the curve tells you whether it's an overestimate or underestimate*

'State whether the estimate in (i) is an overestimate or an underestimate, giving a reason for your answer.'

Looking back at the sketch of the curve:

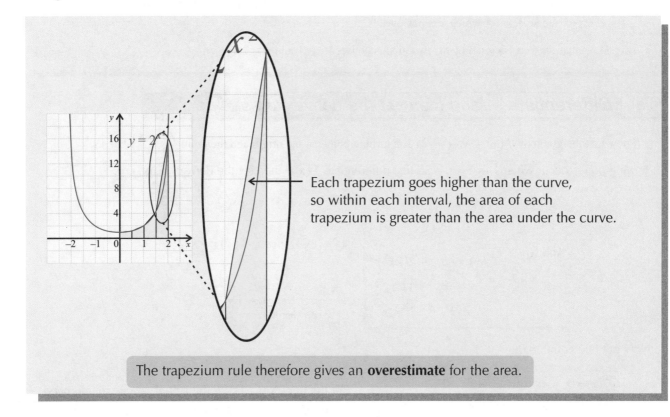

Each trapezium goes higher than the curve, so within each interval, the area of each trapezium is greater than the area under the curve.

The trapezium rule therefore gives an **overestimate** for the area.

Logarithm 'n' blues

Hate to do this to you, but I'm going to sneakily give you an extra question for practice... and it's on logs. I know, I know, I'm a wicked person, but I'm sure you'll rise to the challenge. It'll be over soon.

You can see on the graph of $y = 2^{x^2}$ that the line goes through the point (2, 16).

See if you can work backwards from $2^{x^2} = 16$, using logs, to show that $x = 2$ is a solution. I'll give you a few seconds to think about it...

La la la, la la la-la la la la la, la la la-la la...   That's Kylie, by the way.

Right then.
Take logs of both sides (to the base 2 so you can bring that x^2 down):

Use the law of logs:

$$2^{x^2} = 16$$

$$\log_2 2^{x^2} = \log_2 16$$

$$x^2 \log_2 2 = \log_2 16 \quad \text{Spot that } \log_2 2 \text{ is 1 (because } 2^1 = 2).$$

$$x^2 = \log_2 16 \quad \text{Spot that } \log_2 16 \text{ is 4 (because } 2^4 = 16).$$

$$x^2 = 4$$

$$x = \pm 2 \quad \text{Remember the '±' — the graph is symmetrical about the y-axis.}$$

All over. See how clever you are? You can take anything I throw at you.

Paper 2 Q6 — Integration

6 (i) (a) Show that the graph of $f(x) = -x^2(x-2)$ has turning points at the origin and the point $\left(\frac{4}{3}, \frac{32}{27}\right)$. **[3]**

(b) Sketch the graph of $f(x)$, marking in any turning points and points where it crosses the axes. **[2]**

(ii) The function $g(x)$ is defined by $g(x) = 2-x$. Given that the graphs of $f(x)$ and $g(x)$ meet at $x=1$, sketch the graph of $g(x)$ on the same set of axes you used in part (i), marking in the coordinates of the two points of intersection for which x is positive. **[3]**

(iii) Show that the area enclosed by the two graphs between $x=1$ and $x=2$ is $\frac{5}{12}$. **[4]**

(i)(a) | Differentiate — and then set the derivative equal to Zero

'Show that the graph of $f(x) = -x^2(x-2)$ has turning points at the origin and the point $\left(\frac{4}{3}, \frac{32}{27}\right)$.'

<u>Turning points</u> occur when $f'(x) = 0$. So first differentiate $f(x)$, then set the derivative to <u>zero</u>.

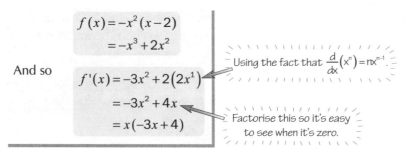

$$f(x) = -x^2(x-2)$$
$$= -x^3 + 2x^2$$

And so
$$f'(x) = -3x^2 + 2(2x^1)$$

Using the fact that $\frac{d}{dx}(x^n) = nx^{n-1}$.

$$= -3x^2 + 4x$$

$$= x(-3x+4)$$

Factorise this so it's easy to see when it's zero.

Now put f'(x) equal to 0:

$$f'(x) = 0 \implies x(-3x+4) = 0$$
$$\implies x = 0 \text{ or } x = \frac{4}{3}$$

So there are turning points at $x = 0$ and $x = \frac{4}{3}$.

But the question asks for the actual <u>points</u>, so you need to find the y-coordinates too, i.e. $f(0)$ and $f\left(\frac{4}{3}\right)$:

$$f(0) = 0, \text{ and } f\left(\frac{4}{3}\right) = -\left(\frac{4}{3}\right)^2\left(\frac{4}{3} - 2\right) = -\frac{16}{9}\left(-\frac{2}{3}\right) = \frac{32}{27}.$$

So the turning points are $(0,0)$ (i.e. the <u>origin</u>) and $\left(\frac{4}{3}, \frac{32}{27}\right)$.

(i)(b) | Sketching f(x) — it's a Cubic

'Sketch the graph of $f(x)$, marking in any turning points and points where it crosses the axes.'

$$f(x) = -x^2(x-2) = -x^3 + 2x^2$$

There's basically three things you need to know to draw this graph:

1. <u>What shape is the graph?</u>

   f(x) is a <u>cubic</u> function, and the coefficient of x^3 is <u>negative</u> (−1) — so it goes from <u>top-left</u> to <u>bottom-right</u>.

   (<u>Or you can work it out:</u>   as x goes towards +∞, $-x^3$ goes towards −∞ and as x goes towards −∞, $-x^3$ goes towards ∞.)

2. <u>Where does it cross the x-axis?</u>

   Just put f(x) equal to 0:

   $$f(x) = -x^2(x-2) = 0 \implies x = 0 \text{ and } x = 2$$

3. <u>Where are the turning points?</u>

   We already know these from part i(a). Don't forget to mark them on.

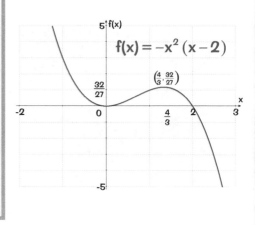

Paper 2 Q6 — Integration

(ii) Sketch a **Straight** line on the **Same** pair of axes

'$g(x)$ is defined by $g(x) = 2 - x$. Given that the graphs of $f(x)$ and $g(x)$ meet at $x = 1$, sketch the graph of $g(x)$ on the same set of axes you used in part (i), marking in the coordinates of the two points of intersection for which x is positive.'

You've got to stick g(x), which is just a straight line, on your graph.
So all you do is <u>plot</u> 2 points and draw a straight line through them.
The best points to choose are where it <u>crosses</u> the x- and y- axes.

> g(x) crosses the: <u>y-axis</u> at y = 2 (just put x = 0),
> and the <u>x-axis</u> at x = 2 (just set g(x) = 0).

The question asks you to mark on the 2 points where f(x) and g(x) meet.

> It tells you that they meet at x=1. And since $f(1) = -1^2(1-2) = 1$,
> the two graphs cross at the point (1,1).
> You can see the other point just by looking at the graph. It's (2,0).

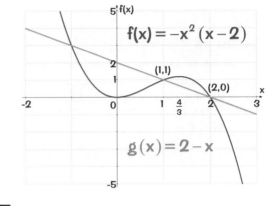

$f(x) = -x^2(x - 2)$

(1,1)

(2,0)

$g(x) = 2 - x$

(iii) Find the **Area** between the curve and the line

'Show that the area enclosed by the two graphs between $x = 1$ and $x = 2$ is $\frac{5}{12}$.'

Without a <u>graph</u>, this part of the question would be pretty tricky — but with the graph you drew in part (ii), you can see exactly which area you need to find. It also helps you to see <u>how</u> you need to go about finding it.

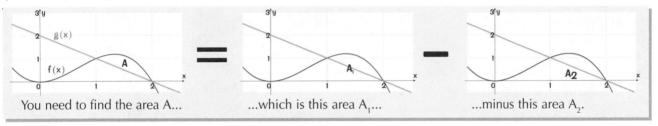

You need to find the area A...   ...which is this area A_1...   ...minus this area A_2.

To find areas under curves, you need to <u>integrate</u>. So...

Area A_1 is:
$$A_1 = \int_1^2 (-x^3 + 2x^2)\,dx$$
$$= \left[-\frac{x^4}{4} + \frac{2x^3}{3} \right]_1^2$$
$$= \left(-\frac{2^4}{4} + \frac{2 \times 2^3}{3} \right) - \left(-\frac{1^4}{4} + \frac{2 \times 1^3}{3} \right)$$
$$= \left(-4 + \frac{16}{3} \right) - \left(-\frac{1}{4} + \frac{2}{3} \right) = \frac{-48+64+3-8}{12} = \frac{11}{12}$$

$$\int_1^2 x^n\,dx = \left[\frac{x^{n+1}}{n+1} \right]_1^2$$

Never rush this bit as it's easy to lose a minus sign.

> Or you could do it this way:
> $$A = \int_1^2 (-x^3 + 2x^2 - (2-x))\,dx$$
> See page 46 for more info.

The area A_2 is a <u>triangle</u>, and the quickest way to find its area is to use the formula: $Area = \frac{1}{2} base \times height$.

And the area A_2 is:
$$A_2 = \frac{1}{2} \times 1 \times 1$$
$$= \frac{1}{2}$$

You could integrate to find the area under the straight line — but this is quicker and easier.

And the area you need is just $A_1 - A_2$:

So the area <u>enclosed</u> by the curves between $x = 1$ and $x = 2$ is:
$$A = A_1 - A_2$$
$$= \frac{11}{12} - \frac{1}{2} = \frac{11-6}{12} = \frac{5}{12}$$

I've got a bad feeling about this...

This is a real meaty question, which makes it look horrendous — but a quick think and a quick sketch before you start will be dead useful (for part (iii) especially). And as long as you've had plenty of practice with the little tricks you need to use (e.g. differentiating to find turning points, sketching graphs, integrating to finding areas under graphs), you'll be all right.

Paper 2 Q7 — Graph Transformations

7 (i) Sketch the graph of $y = 1 - (x - 2)^2$, marking carefully the points where the curve meets the coordinate axes. [3]

(ii) Using the same axes, sketch the graph of $y = 1.5x - 2$. [2]

(iii) Prove that the x-coordinates of the points of intersection of the two graphs satisfy the equation

$2x^2 - 5x + 2 = 0$. [3]

(iv) Solve this equation to find the coordinates of the points of intersection of the two graphs. [3]

(i) | Work out intercepts and turning point... then do a sketch

'Sketch the graph of $y = 1 - (x - 2)^2$, marking carefully the points where the curve meets the coordinate axes.'

Before you go any further, you want to <u>rearrange the expression</u> so that it's a clear '$ax^2 + bx + c$' quadratic.

You can multiply through by –1 or leave the "–" sign outside the brackets so it's easier to factorise.

$y = 1 - (x - 2)^2 = 1 - (x^2 - 4x + 4)$

$y = -(x^2 - 4x + 3)$

To draw the graph you need to work out <u>three things</u>:

① the <u>x-intercepts</u>, where $y = 0$.

$0 = -(x^2 - 4x + 3)$
Factorising gives: $(x - 3)(x - 1) = 0$
So $x = 3$ or $x = 1$
So the graph cuts the x-axis at $x = 3$ and $x = 1$, i.e. at (3, 0) and (1, 0)

② the <u>y-intercept</u>, where $x = 0$.

$y = -[0^2 - (4 \times 0) + 3] = -3$

So the graph cuts the y-axis
at $y = -3$, i.e. at (0, –3)

③ the <u>turning point</u>, where the <u>gradient = 0</u>.

<u>Differentiate</u> the expression for y to get the gradient:
$y = -(x^2 - 4x + 3) = -x^2 + 4x - 3$

$\dfrac{dy}{dx} = -2x + 4 = 0$ at turning point

which means $x = 2$ and $y = -[2^2 - (4 \times 2) + 3] = 1$

So, the turning point is at (2, 1).

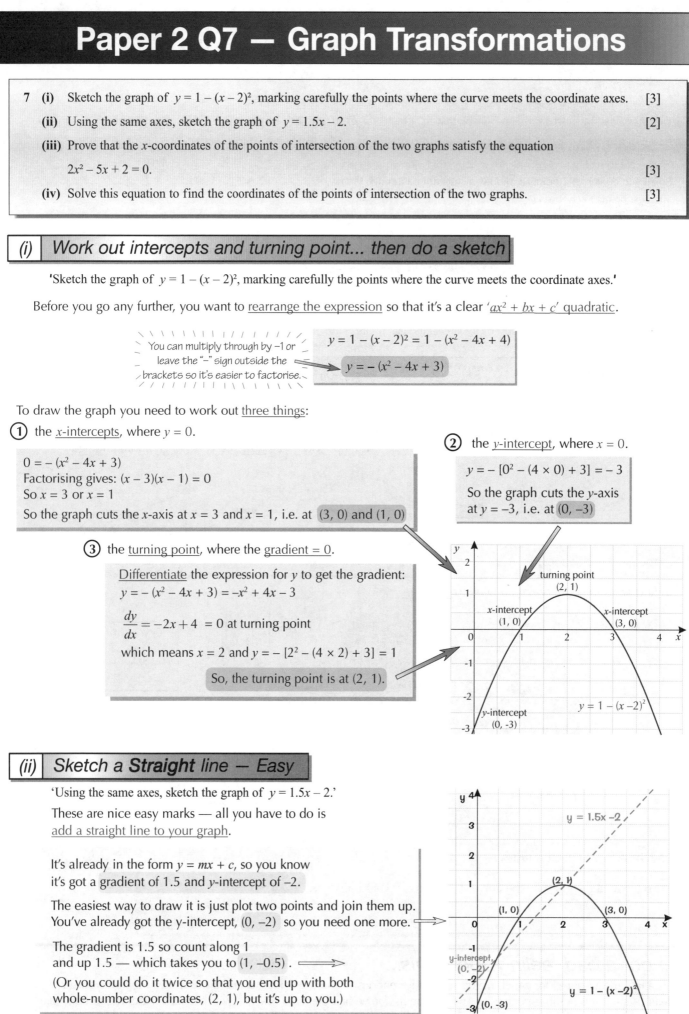

(ii) | Sketch a **Straight** line — Easy

'Using the same axes, sketch the graph of $y = 1.5x - 2$.'

These are nice easy marks — all you have to do is
<u>add a straight line to your graph</u>.

It's already in the form $y = mx + c$, so you know
it's got a gradient of 1.5 and y-intercept of –2.

The easiest way to draw it is just plot two points and join them up.
You've already got the y-intercept, (0, –2) so you need one more.

The gradient is 1.5 so count along 1
and up 1.5 — which takes you to (1, –0.5).

(Or you could do it twice so that you end up with both
whole-number coordinates, (2, 1), but it's up to you.)

Paper 2 Q7 — Graph Transformations

(iii) Equate and rearrange

'Prove that the x-coordinates of the points of intersection of the two graphs satisfy the equation $2x^2 - 5x + 2 = 0$.'

When the x- and y-values of each graph are the same, it means that the two lines go through the <u>same point</u> — in other words they <u>cross</u>.

To find out where this happens, you treat them as <u>simultaneous equations</u>:

You've got 2 equations:
$$y = -(x^2 - 4x + 3) \quad — (i)$$
$$y = 1.5x - 2 \quad — (ii)$$

At the point where they cross, the y-value of equation (i) is equal to the y-value of equation (ii), which gives:

$$-(x^2 - 4x + 3) = 1.5x - 2$$
$$-x^2 + 4x - 3 = 1.5x - 2$$

Rearrange until you get what the question asks for:
$$-x^2 + 2.5x - 1 = 0$$
$$2x^2 - 5x + 2 = 0 \quad \text{(exactly what you want)}$$

(iv) Solve a quadratic — wahey

'Solve this equation to find the coordinates of the points of intersection of the two graphs.'

On the home straight now — <u>solve the quadratic</u> in x (easy) then <u>substitute</u> the answer back in to find y. And I'm sure you're so familiar with solving quadratics by now that you could do them with your feet.

But just in case...

Check whether it'll <u>factorise</u> (or just use the formula if you prefer).

This is the fiddly bit where you have to try a few combinations — check back in Core 1 if you've forgotten.

$$2x^2 - 5x + 2 = 0$$
$$(2x - 1)(x - 2) = 0$$
$$(2x - 1) = 0 \text{ or } (x - 2) = 0$$

So the two possible solutions are: $x = \dfrac{1}{2}$ and $x = 2$

<u>Using the formula:</u>
$$y = \frac{-b \pm \sqrt{b^2 - 4ac}}{2a}$$
$$= \frac{5 \pm \sqrt{(-5)^2 - 4 \times 2 \times 2}}{2 \times 2}$$
$$= \frac{5 \pm \sqrt{25 - 16}}{4} = \frac{5 \pm 3}{4}$$
$$= \frac{1}{2} \text{ or } 2$$

Substitute these x-values back into the original equations to find the y-values.

The original equations were:
$$y = -(x^2 - 4x + 3) \quad — (i)$$
$$y = 1.5x - 2 \quad — (ii)$$

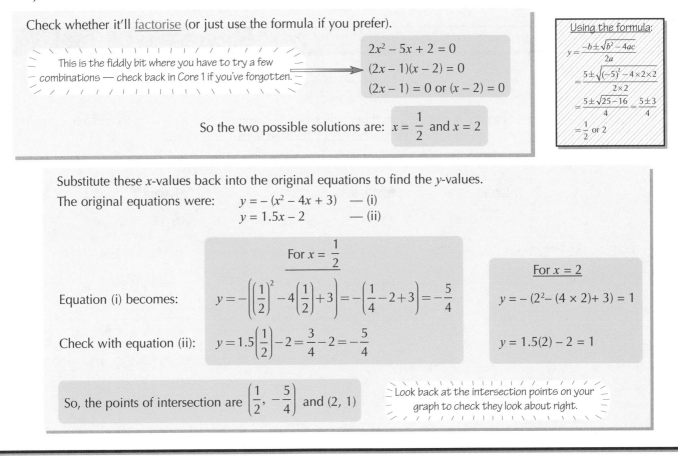

For $x = \dfrac{1}{2}$

Equation (i) becomes:
$$y = -\left(\left(\frac{1}{2}\right)^2 - 4\left(\frac{1}{2}\right) + 3\right) = -\left(\frac{1}{4} - 2 + 3\right) = -\frac{5}{4}$$

Check with equation (ii):
$$y = 1.5\left(\frac{1}{2}\right) - 2 = \frac{3}{4} - 2 = -\frac{5}{4}$$

For $x = 2$
$$y = -(2^2 - (4 \times 2) + 3) = 1$$
$$y = 1.5(2) - 2 = 1$$

So, the points of intersection are $\left(\dfrac{1}{2}, -\dfrac{5}{4}\right)$ and $(2, 1)$

Look back at the intersection points on your graph to check they look about right.

What a beaut...

You see — this is the kind of question you really want to come up in your exam. The only part of that question that you couldn't do at GCSE was differentiating the quadratic to get the turning point. OK so you wouldn't get a question quite that long at GCSE, but most of the actual *maths* is <u>no harder</u>. So take comfort, O ye of little faith — AS Maths isn't *all* horrible.

Paper 2 Q8 — Geometric Progressions

8   For the series with second term –2 and common ratio $-\frac{1}{2}$, find:

   (i)   the first term   [2]

   (ii)   the first seven terms   [3]

   (iii)   the sum of the first seven terms   [3]

   (iv)   the sum to infinity   [3]

(i)   Use the Common Ratio to find the First Term

'For the series with second term –2 and common ratio $-\frac{1}{2}$, find the first term'

The question gives you a couple of bits of information:

    (i) The second term in the geometric series, $u_2 = -2$.

    (ii) The common ratio, $r = -\frac{1}{2}$.

The common ratio is $\frac{u_{n+1}}{u_n}$. It's the same for any pair of terms next to each other in the sequence — including the first and second terms.

The first term (u_1) is called 'a'

So just plug in the values and solve for u_1:

$$\frac{u_2}{u_1} = \frac{u_2}{a} = -\frac{1}{2}$$

$$a = -2u_2 = -2(-2) = 4$$

(ii)   Sub your numbers into the Formula for the nth term of a Geometric Series

'find the first seven terms'

There are two ways of doing this.

Method 1:   Use the first term from part (i) and multiply it by the common ratio to get the second term, then multiply the second term by the common ratio to get the third term... and so on.

OR   Method 2:   You can substitute the first term and the relevant *n*-value into the nth term formula — $ar^{(n-1)}$.

Term	n	Method 1	Method 2		Value
u_1	1	$a = 4$	$a = 4$	$=$	4
u_2	2	$ar = u_1 \times -\frac{1}{2} = 4 \times -\frac{1}{2}$	$ar = 4 \times \left(-\frac{1}{2}\right)^1$	$=$	-2
u_3	3	$(ar) \times r = u_2 \times -\frac{1}{2} = -2 \times -\frac{1}{2}$	$ar^2 = 4 \times \left(-\frac{1}{2}\right)^2$	$=$	1
u_4	4	$(ar^2) \times r = u_3 \times -\frac{1}{2} = 1 \times -\frac{1}{2}$	$ar^3 = 4 \times \left(-\frac{1}{2}\right)^3$	$=$	$-\frac{1}{2}$
u_5	5	$(ar^3) \times r = u_4 \times -\frac{1}{2} = -\frac{1}{2} \times -\frac{1}{2}$	$ar^4 = 4 \times \left(-\frac{1}{2}\right)^4$	$=$	$\frac{1}{4}$
u_6	6	$(ar^4) \times r = u_5 \times -\frac{1}{2} = \frac{1}{4} \times -\frac{1}{2}$	$ar^5 = 4 \times \left(-\frac{1}{2}\right)^5$	$=$	$-\frac{1}{8}$
u_7	7	$(ar^5) \times r = u_6 \times -\frac{1}{2} = -\frac{1}{8} \times -\frac{1}{2}$	$ar^6 = 4 \times \left(-\frac{1}{2}\right)^6$	$=$	$\frac{1}{16}$
.	.	.	.		.
n^th	n	$ar^{(n-2)} \times r$	$ar^{(n-1)}$	$=$	$ar^{(n-1)}$

1st term × r

2nd term × r

3rd term × r

With Method 1, each term is made up of the previous term multiplied by r.

With Method 2, each consecutive term is just the first term multiplied by a higher power of r

Paper 2 Q8 — Geometric Progressions

(iii) | Put n, a and r into the Sum of a Geometric Series Formula

'find the sum of the first seven terms'

Again, you've got a choice of how you work out this question.

Method 1: The obvious way is to <u>write down all seven terms</u> that you've just worked out for part (ii) and <u>add them all together</u>:

S_7 = sum of the first 7 terms

$$= 4 - 2 + 1 - \frac{1}{2} + \frac{1}{4} - \frac{1}{8} + \frac{1}{16} = \frac{43}{16} = 2\frac{11}{16}$$

Method 2: But rather than doing a long sum of seven different terms, you could just put your a, r and n values into the <u>formula for the sum of a geometric series</u>:

$$S_n = \frac{a(1 - r^n)}{1 - r}$$

The advantage of this method is that it won't carry through any errors you might have made in part (ii). So it's a handy formula to know.

Write down your a, r and n values so they're clearly visible and you won't get confused:

it's the sum of the first seven terms that you're interested in so n = 7

$a = 4$
$n = 7$
$r = -\frac{1}{2}$

Now, put them into the formula, do a little dance and bit of fiddling around and hey presto, you've got your answer:

$a = 4$ $\qquad$ $n = 7$

$$S_n = \frac{4\left(1 - \left(-\frac{1}{2}\right)^7\right)}{1 - \left(-\frac{1}{2}\right)} = \frac{4\left(1 + \frac{1}{128}\right)}{\frac{3}{2}} = \frac{2}{3} \times 4\left(\frac{129}{128}\right) = \frac{43}{16} = 2\frac{11}{16}$$

$r = -\frac{1}{2}$

Dividing by a fraction is the same thing as multiplying by the fraction turned on its head.

(iv) | Simplify the numerator and plug in a and r

'find the sum to infinity'

Don't worry, this question sounds worse than it is. You <u>don't</u> have to work out every term from 1 to infinity (ha!) but you <u>will</u> have to use that formula for working out the sum to infinity of a geometric series (see p.24):

$$S_\infty = \frac{a}{1 - r}$$

The tricky bit is remembering the formula. After that, the rest of the question is just a case of plugging in the numbers and fiddling around again:

$$S_\infty = \frac{a}{1 - r} = \frac{4}{1 - \left(-\frac{1}{2}\right)} = \frac{4}{\frac{3}{2}} = \frac{2}{3} \times 4 = \frac{8}{3} = 2\frac{2}{3}$$

But if your mind goes blank in the exam and you can't remember the infinity sum equation, all's not lost. It's pretty easy to work out the formula for a sum to infinity from the general sum equation. All you need to do is look at what happens to the r^n $\left(-\frac{1}{2}\right)^n$, term as n tends to ∞. The higher the n value, the more times you multiply $-\frac{1}{2}$ by itself. The more times you do this, the smaller the resulting number. $\left(-\frac{1}{2}\right)^\infty$ is a tiny, tiny number. In fact, it's so small, you can just ignore it:

$$a(1 - 0) = a \quad \Rightarrow \quad S_\infty = \frac{a(1 - r_\infty)}{1 - r} = \frac{a}{1 - r}$$

Sum to infinity — but not beyond...

Andit's no way, never. No way never, no more. And I'll do the geometric progression question... no never, no more.

Answers

Section One — Algebra and Functions

1) a) x^8 b) a^{15} c) x^6 d) a^8 e) x^4y^3z f) $\dfrac{b^2c^5}{a}$

2) a) 4 b) 2 c) 8 d) 1 e) $1/7$

3) a)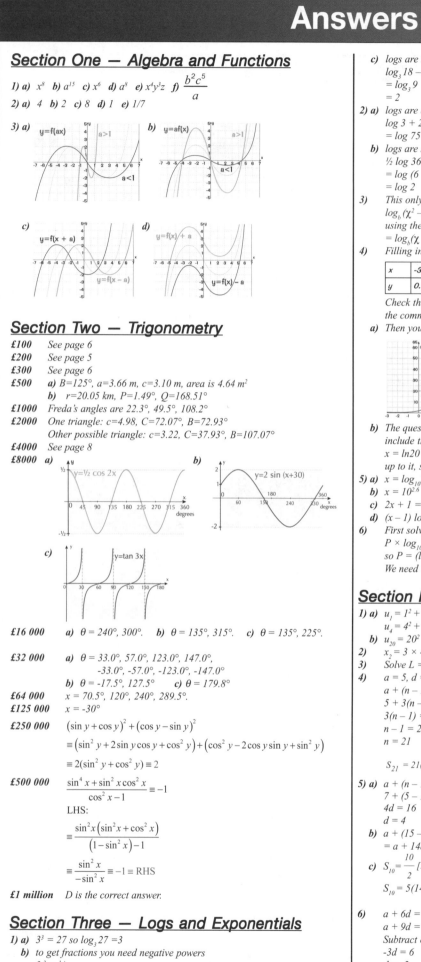

b)

c)

d)

Section Two — Trigonometry

£100   See page 6
£200   See page 5
£300   See page 6
£500   a) $B=125°$, $a=3.66$ m, $c=3.10$ m, area is 4.64 m^2
        b) $r=20.05$ km, $P=1.49°$, $Q=168.51°$
£1000   Freda's angles are $22.3°$, $49.5°$, $108.2°$
£2000   One triangle: $c=4.98$, $C=72.07°$, $B=72.93°$
        Other possible triangle: $c=3.22$, $C=37.93°$, $B=107.07°$
£4000   See page 8
£8000   a)   b)

c)

£16 000   a) $\theta = 240°$, $300°$. b) $\theta = 135°$, $315°$. c) $\theta = 135°$, $225°$.

£32 000   a) $\theta = 33.0°$, $57.0°$, $123.0°$, $147.0°$,
             $-33.0°$, $-57.0°$, $-123.0°$, $-147.0°$
          b) $\theta = -17.5°$, $127.5°$ c) $\theta = 179.8°$
£64 000 $x = 70.5°$, $120°$, $240°$, $289.5°$.
£125 000 $x = -30°$
£250 000 $\left(\sin y + \cos y\right)^2 + \left(\cos y - \sin y\right)^2$
          $\equiv \left(\sin^2 y + 2\sin y\cos y + \cos^2 y\right) + \left(\cos^2 y - 2\cos y\sin y + \sin^2 y\right)$
          $\equiv 2(\sin^2 y + \cos^2 y) \equiv 2$
£500 000 $\dfrac{\sin^4 x + \sin^2 x\cos^2 x}{\cos^2 x - 1} \equiv -1$
          LHS:
          $\equiv \dfrac{\sin^2 x\left(\sin^2 x + \cos^2 x\right)}{\left(1 - \sin^2 x\right) - 1}$
          $\equiv \dfrac{\sin^2 x}{-\sin^2 x} \equiv -1 \equiv$ RHS
£1 million D is the correct answer.

Section Three — Logs and Exponentials

1) a) $3^3 = 27$ so $\log_3 27 = 3$
   b) to get fractions you need negative powers
      $3^{-3} = 1/27$
      $\log_3(1/27) = -3$

c) logs are subtracted so divide
   $\log_3 18 - \log_3 2 = \log_3(18 \div 2)$
   $= \log_3 9$
   $= 2$ $(3^2 = 9)$

2) a) logs are added so you multiply — remember $2\log 5 = \log 5^2$
      $\log 3 + 2\log 5 = \log(3 \times 5^2)$
      $= \log 75$
   b) logs are subtracted so you divide and the power half means square root
      $\frac{1}{2}\log 36 - \log 3 = \log(36^{\frac{1}{2}} \div 3)$
      $= \log(6 \div 3)$
      $= \log 2$

3) This only looks tricky because of the algebra, just remember the laws
   $\log_b(\chi^2 - 1) - \log_b(\chi - 1) = \log_b\{(\chi^2 - 1)/(\chi - 1)\}$
   using the difference of two squares $(\chi^2 - 1) = (\chi - 1)(\chi + 1)$ and cancelling
   $= \log_b(\chi + 1)$

4) Filling in the answers is just a case of using the calculator

x	-3	-2	-1	0	1	2	3
y	0.0156	0.0625	0.25	1	4	16	64

Check that it agrees with what we know about the graphs. It goes through the common point $(0,1)$, and it follows the standard shape.
   a) Then you just need to draw the graph, and use a scale that's just right.

   b) The question tells you to use the graph to get your answer, so you'll need to include the construction lines, but check the answer with the calculator.
      $x = \ln 20 / \ln 4 = 2.16$, but you can't justify this accuracy if your graph's not up to it, so 2.2 is a good estimate.
5) a) $x = \log_{10}240 / \log_{10}10 = \log_{10}240 = 2.380$
   b) $x = 10^{2.6} = 398.1$
   c) $2x + 1 = \log_{10}1500 = 3.176$, so $2x = 2.176$, so $x = 1.088$
   d) $(x - 1)\log 4 = \log 200$, so $x - 1 = \log 200 / \log 4 = 3.822$, so $x = 4.822$
6) First solve for $1.5^P = 1,000,000$
   $P \times \log_{10}1.5 = \log_{10}1,000,000$,
   so $P = (\log_{10}1,000,000) / (\log_{10}1.5) = 34.07$.
   We need the next biggest integer, so this will be $P = 35$.

Section Four — Sequences and Series

1) a) $u_1 = 1^2 + 3 = 4$; $u_2 = 2^2 + 3 = 7$; $u_3 = 3^2 + 3 = 12$;
      $u_4 = 4^2 + 3 = 19$
   b) $u_{20} = 20^2 + 3 = 403$
2) $x_2 = 3 \times 4 - 2 = 10$; $x_3 = 3 \times 10 - 2 = 28$; $x_4 = 3 \times 28 - 2 = 82$
3) Solve $L = 3L/4 + 7$, i.e. $L/4 = 7$, i.e. $L = 28$
4) $a = 5$, $d = 3$, $l = 65$
   $a + (n - 1)d = l$
   $5 + 3(n - 1) = 65$
   $3(n - 1) = 60$
   $n - 1 = 20$
   $n = 21$

   $S_{21} = 21\left(\dfrac{5 + 65}{2}\right) = 735$
5) a) $a + (n - 1)d = $ nth term
      $7 + (5 - 1)d = 23$
      $4d = 16$
      $d = 4$
   b) $a + (15 - 1)d$ is 15th term
      $= a + 14d = 7 + 14 \times 4 = 63$
   c) $S_{10} = \dfrac{10}{2}[2 \times 7 + (10 - 1) \times 4]$
      $S_{10} = 5(14 + 36) = 250$
6) $a + 6d = 36$
   $a + 9d = 30$
   Subtract one equation from the other:
   $-3d = 6$
   $d = -2$
   Plug d into one of the original equations:
   $a + 6 \times -2 = 36$

Answers

$a - 12 = 36$
$\underline{a = 48}$

$S_5 = \frac{5}{2}[2 \times 48 + (5-1) \times -2]$

$S_5 = \frac{5}{2}(96-8) \ \underline{=220}$

$n^{th} \text{ term} = a + (n-1)d$
$= 48 + (n-1) \times -2$
$= 48 - 2n + 2 = \underline{50 - 2n}$

7) a) $\sum_{n=1}^{20}(3n-1) = 2 + 5 + 8 + ... + 59 = 20(\frac{2+59}{2}) = 610$

b) $\sum_{n=1}^{10}(48-5n) = 43 + 38 + 33 + ... + -2 = 10(\frac{43+-2}{2}) = 205$

8) $a = 2, r = -3$
$10^{th} \text{ term}, u_{10} = ar^9$
$= 2 \times (-3)^9 = -39366$

9) a) $r = 2nd \text{ term} \div 1^{st} \text{ term}$
$r = 12 \div 24 = \frac{1}{2}$

b) $7^{th} \text{ term} = ar^6$
$= 24 \times (\frac{1}{2})^6$
$= 0.375 \ (\text{or } \frac{3}{8})$

c) $S_\infty = \frac{a}{1-r} = \frac{24}{1-\frac{1}{2}} = 48$

10) $G.P. - 2, 6, ... \quad a = 2, r = 3$
$5^{th} \text{ term is } ar^4 = 2 \times 3^4 = \underline{162}$
$A.P. - 2, 6, ... \quad a=2, d=4$
You need $a + (n-1)d = 162$
$2 + (n-1)4 = 162$
$4(n-1) = 160$
$n - 1 = 40$
$\underline{n = 41}$ i.e. the 41st term of the AP is equal to the 5th term of the G.P.

11) $(2 + 3x)^5 = 2^5(1 + \frac{3}{2}x)^5$

$= 2^5[1 + \frac{5}{1}(\frac{3}{2}x) + \frac{5 \times 4}{1 \times 2}(\frac{3}{2}x)^2 + ...]$

x^2 term is $2^5 \times \frac{5 \times 4}{1 \times 2}(\frac{3}{2})^2 x^2$, so coefficient is $2^5 \times \frac{5 \times 4}{1 \times 2} \times \frac{3^2}{2^2} = 720$

Section Five — Differentiation

1 a) $\frac{dy}{dx} = nx^{n-1} = -4x^{-5}$

b) $\frac{dy}{dx} = nx^{n-1} = (3)(\frac{1}{2})x^{-\frac{1}{2}} = \frac{3}{2}x^{-\frac{1}{2}}$

c) Apply the rule to each term one by one:
$f'(x) = (4)(2)x^1 - (3)(-3)x^{-4}$
$f'(x) = 8x + 9x^{-4}$

2 a) i) First write using index notation:
$y = 3x^{\frac{1}{2}} + 4x^{-1}$
Now differentiate each term using the normal rule:
$\frac{dy}{dx} = (3)(\frac{1}{2})x^{-\frac{1}{2}} + (4)(-1)x^{-2}$
$= \frac{3}{2}x^{-\frac{1}{2}} - 4x^{-2}$

ii) To get the gradient at (4,7) work out $\frac{dy}{dx}$ when $x = 4$:
$\frac{dy}{dx} = (\frac{3}{2})(4^{-\frac{1}{2}}) - (4)(4^{-2})$
$= (\frac{3}{2})(\frac{1}{2}) - (4)(\frac{1}{16})$
$= \frac{3}{4} - \frac{1}{4} = \frac{1}{2}$

b) i) Using index notation: $y = 2x^{-2} + 3x^{-3}$
Differentiating each term one by one:
$\frac{dy}{dx} = (2)(-2)x^{-3} + (3)(-3)x^{-4}$
$= -4x^{-3} - 9x^{-4}$

ii) To get the gradient at (1,5) work out $\frac{dy}{dx}$ when $x = 1$:
$\frac{dy}{dx} = (-4)(1^{-3}) - (9)(1^{-4})$
$= -4 - 9 = -13$

3 a) To verify that the graphs meet at (1,3) you only need to put $x = 1$ into each equation and show that the y values are both 3.
For $y = 4 - x$, at $x = 1$:
$4 - x = 4 - 1 = \underline{3}$

For $y = \frac{2}{\sqrt{x}} + 1$, at $x = 1$:

$\frac{2}{\sqrt{x}} + 1 = \frac{2}{1} + 1 = \underline{3}$

Therefore the graphs must intersect at (1,3).

b) To differentiate, write in index form:
$y = 2x^{-\frac{1}{2}} + 1$
Now differentiate:
$\frac{dy}{dx} = (2)(-\frac{1}{2})x^{-\frac{3}{2}} = -x^{-\frac{3}{2}}$

c) To find the gradient of $y = \frac{2}{\sqrt{x}} + 1$ at (1,3), substitute $x = 1$ into the
formula: $\frac{dy}{dx} = -(1^{-\frac{3}{2}}) = -1$

Section Six — Integration

1) a) $2x^5 + C$ **b)** $\frac{-2}{x^2} + C$ **c)** $\frac{3}{4}x^4 + \frac{2}{3}x^3 + C$

d) $3x^{\frac{4}{3}} + C = 3\sqrt[3]{x^4} + C$ **e)** $x^6 + \frac{2}{x} + \frac{2}{3}x^{\frac{3}{2}} + C$

2) $y = \frac{2}{3}x^{\frac{3}{2}} - \frac{2}{x} + C$

Putting $x = 1$ and $y = 0$ gives: $0 = \frac{2}{3} - 2 + C$

so $C = \frac{4}{3}$ and the required curve is $y = \frac{2}{3}x^{\frac{3}{2}} - \frac{2}{x} + \frac{4}{3}$

3) a) $\int_1^2 \frac{8}{x^5} + \frac{3}{\sqrt{x}}dx = \int_1^2 8x^{-5} + 3x^{-\frac{1}{2}}dx$

$= \left[\frac{8x^{-4}}{-4} + \frac{3x^{\frac{1}{2}}}{\frac{1}{2}}\right]_1^2 = \left[-\frac{2}{x^4} + 6\sqrt{x}\right]_1^2$

$= \left[(-\frac{1}{8} + 6\sqrt{2}) - (-2 + 6)\right] = -\frac{33}{8} + 6\sqrt{2}$

b) $\int_1^6 \frac{3}{y^2} \, dy = \int_1^6 3y^{-2} \, dy = \left[-\frac{3}{y}\right]_1^6$

$= \left[\left(-\frac{3}{6}\right) - \left(-\frac{3}{1}\right)\right] = \frac{5}{2}$

4) $\int_1^8 y \, dx = \int_1^8 x^{-\frac{1}{3}} \, dx = \left[\frac{3}{2}x^{\frac{2}{3}}\right]_1^8$

$= \left[\left(\frac{3}{2} \times 8^{\frac{2}{3}}\right) - \left(\frac{3}{2} \times 1^{\frac{2}{3}}\right)\right] = \left(\frac{3}{2} \times 4\right) - \left(\frac{3}{2} \times 1\right) = \frac{9}{2}$

5) a) $x_0 = 0: \quad y_0 = \sqrt{9} = 3$
$x_1 = 1: \quad y_1 = \sqrt{8} = 2.8284$
$x_2 = 2: \quad y_2 = \sqrt{5} = 2.2361$
$x_3 = 3: \quad y_3 = \sqrt{0} = 0$

$h = \frac{(3-0)}{3} = 1$

$\int_a^b y dx = \frac{1}{2}[(3+0) + 2(2.8284 + 2.2361)] = 6.5645 \approx 6.56$

b) $x_0 = 0.2: \quad y_0 = 0.2^{0.04} = 0.93765$
$x_1 = 0.4: \quad y_1 = 0.4^{0.16} = 0.86363$
$x_2 = 0.6: \quad y_2 = 0.6^{0.36} = 0.83202$
$x_3 = 0.8: \quad y_3 = 0.8^{0.64} = 0.86692$
$x_4 = 1: \quad y_4 = 1^1 = 1$
$x_5 = 1.2: \quad y_5 = 1.2^{1.44} = 1.30023$

$h = \frac{(1.2 - 0.2)}{5} = 0.2$

$\int_a^b y dx \approx \frac{0.2}{2}[(0.93765 + 1.30023) + 2(0.86363 + 0.83202 + 0.86692 + 1)]$

$= 0.1 \times 9.36302 \approx 0.9363$

Index